Learning the UNIX Operating System

Learning the
UNIX Operating System

Grace Todino, John Strang,
and Jerry Peek

O'Reilly & Associates, Inc.

Cambridge • *Köln* • *Paris* • *Sebastopol* • *Tokyo*

Learning the UNIX Operating System

by Grace Todino, John Strang, and Jerry Peek

Editor: Tim O'Reilly

Production Editor: Leslie Chalmers

Printing History:

1986:	First Edition. Written by Grace Todino and John Strang.
1987:	Second Edition. Revised by Tim O'Reilly.
April 1989:	Minor corrections.
August 1993:	Third Edition. Additions and revisions by Jerry Peek.
June 1994:	Minor corrections.

ISBN: 1-56592-060-0   [9/97]

Table of Contents

Figures

Tables

Preface

The UNIX Operating System

An *operating system* is a collection of programs that controls and organizes the resources of a computer system. These resources consist of *hardware* components such as terminals, printers and line printers, and the *software* programs that tell the computer to perform specific tasks.

Most personal computers have single-user operating systems. That is, only one person can use the system at a time, and the system can handle only one task at a time. Most larger systems are multi-user, multi-tasking systems; several terminals are connected to the computer and the operating system manages access to the computer by a community of users. A computer with this kind of operating system can handle many tasks at the same time.

UNIX is a multi-user, multi-tasking operating system originally developed at AT&T Bell Laboratories. It provides programs for editing text, sending electronic mail, preparing tables, performing calculations and many other specialized functions that require separate application programs in other operating systems.

More and more users—writers, scientists, programmers, managers, and others—are using UNIX for jobs such as:

- Text editing and printing

- Document handling and storage

- Programming and software development

- Electronic communication (e-mail, FAX, networking)

- Computer-aided instruction

- Industrial process control

- Business administration

Versions of UNIX

There are many different versions of UNIX. One of the most important is the line of UNIX releases that started at AT&T, the latest being System V Release 4. Other important UNIX versions have come from the University of California at Berkeley; the last is called BSD4.4. Xenix, the most popular microcomputer implementation of UNIX, was originally based on an earlier AT&T release called Version 7, but has since been upgraded and made largely compatible with System V. POSIX is a standard for UNIX-like operating systems. Some of the other major versions include SunOS, Solaris, SCO UNIX, AIX, HP/UX and ULTRIX.

Many versions of UNIX, including System V Release 4, merge earlier AT&T releases with BSD features. As time goes on, merging of UNIX features will probably continue. Although advanced features differ among systems, you should be able to use this introductory handbook regardless of which type of system you have.

Since it started more than 20 years ago, UNIX has grown and changed in a different way from most operating systems. Many early UNIX users were computer and scientific professionals; more than a few of them extended UNIX by adding tools and functionality to do what they needed. UNIX was also used to develop a lot of the powerful networking systems that connect the world. So, whereas most major operating systems were typically developed and controlled by one corporation, UNIX has been developed through a collective effort. This has meant more versions and somewhat more confusion than "standardized" operating systems like MS/DOS. But it has also helped to make UNIX the flexible and incredibly rich operating system that it is today.

UNIX can be used the way it was originally designed, on typewriter-like terminals. Most versions of UNIX can also work with window systems, which allows each user to have more than one "terminal" on a single display. Chapter 2 shows the basics of a window system. All other chapters are for every UNIX user—with or without a window system.

What this Handbook Covers

Learning the UNIX Operating System teaches the basic system utility commands to get you started with UNIX. We've chosen the topics and commands that we feel a new user should learn. Instead of overwhelming you with a barrage of details, we want you to be comfortable in the UNIX environment as soon as possible; therefore, we cover the most useful features of a command instead of detailing all its options. Appendix A lists additional references.

After reading this handbook, you should be able to do these things:

- Log in and log out of your system

- Control the system with control characters

- Send messages to other users

- Manage UNIX files and directories, including listing, creating, copying, printing and removing files, and moving in and out of directories

- Work more efficiently using UNIX pipes, filters and multi-tasking

What's New in the Third Edition

When we first wrote this book, the typical reader shared a single UNIX computer with a group of other users. Each user sat at a simple terminal with a single window to work in. Some computers had basic network connections to other computers.

Now many users have UNIX computers of their own. Displays with multiple windows are replacing simple terminals. Computers are often part of sophisticated networks within the company or around the world. Different versions of UNIX are merging and becoming more alike. At the same time, a new group of users are encountering UNIX as a "second system:" they are getting information from a public-access UNIX computer or connecting from a non-UNIX computer through the Internet network.

To update the book, we've explained common commands for using networks. There's a new chapter about window systems. The section on electronic mail, and other sections throughout the book, have been updated for the newest versions of UNIX.

Format

The following sections describe the conventions used in this handbook.

Commands

We introduce each main concept, then break it down into task-oriented sections. Next we show the best command to use for specific tasks, explain what it does and give the proper syntax for using it. The syntax is given like this:

> **rm** *filename*

Commands appear in **boldface** type (in this example, **rm**). You would type the command exactly as it appears in the example. The variable parts (here *filename*) will appear in *italic* type. You must supply your own value. To enter a command, for example **rm**, type "rm" followed by the name of the file that you want to remove, then press the RETURN key. Throughout this book, the term *enter* means the process of typing the command and pressing RETURN to run the command.

Examples

Examples show what should happen as you enter a command. Some of the examples assume that you have previously created some files. If you haven't, you may not get the results shown.

Examples are set off from the main text in typewriter-style characters. Items that you would type if you were trying the example are shown in bold characters. System messages and responses are printed in normal characters.

Here's an example:

```
% date
Thu Nov  4 13:39:24 EST 1993
%
```

The character "%" is the prompt. To perform this example, you would type "date" and then press RETURN. The **date** command responds "Thu Nov 4 13:39:24 EST 1993".

Problem Checklist

We've included a problem checklist in sections where you may have some trouble. You may skip these parts and go back to them if you have a problem.

Exercises

Each section includes exercises to reinforce what you have read in the text. Follow the exercises, but don't be afraid to experiment on your own.

The exercises have two columns: the left-hand column tells you what to do and the right-hand column tells you how to do it.

For example, a line in the Exercise section near the end of Chapter 1 shows:

Get today's date   Enter **date**

To follow the exercise, you type in the word **date** on your keyboard and then press the RETURN key. The left-hand column tells you what will happen.

After you try the commands, you'll have a better idea of the ones you want to learn more about. You can then look them up in your system's UNIX documentation or use one of the other references listed in Appendix A.

A Note To Our Readers

Nutshell Handbooks are written by people who have gone through a similar learning process as you. Our goal is to share our experience so that you can become more productive in less time.

We update each book periodically. This allows us to incorporate changes suggested to us by our readers. We'd like new users to benefit from your experience as well as ours.

If you have a suggestion or solve a significant problem that our handbook does not cover, please write to us and let us know about it. Include information about your UNIX environment and the computer you use. Our postal address is on the title page; if your system has electronic mail (Chapter 3), you may e-mail your comments to *bookquestions@ora.com*. If we are able to use your suggestion in the next edition of the book, we'll send you a copy of the new edition. You'll have our thanks, along with thanks from future readers of this handbook.

Acknowledgements

Parts of Chapter 2 were adapted from O'Reilly & Associates' *X Window System User's Guide, Volume 3, OSF/Motif Edition,* by Valerie Quercia and Tim O'Reilly. Parts of the Reference List in Appendix A were adapted from *A Selected Bibilography of UNIX & X Books* from O'Reilly & Associates. H. Milton Peek proofread the third edition. Valerie Quercia reviewed the new Chapter 2. Leslie Chalmers copyedited and produced the third edition. Chris Reilly created the graphics. Clairemarie Fisher O'Leary assisted with final production.

1

Getting Started

Working in the UNIX Environment

Before you can start using UNIX and its facilities, the System Administrator has to set up a UNIX account for you. Think of this account as your office—it's your place in the UNIX environment. Other users may also be at work on the same system. At many sites, there will be a whole network of UNIX computers. So in addition to knowing what your account name is, you may also need to know the *hostname* (name) of the computer that has your account.

Each user communicates with the computer from a terminal or a window. To get into the UNIX environment, you first connect to the UNIX computer. (You may have a terminal that's already connected to the computer.) Next, you start a session by logging in to your UNIX account. Logging in does two things: it identifies which user is in a specific session, and it tells the computer that you are ready to begin working. When your work is finished, you log out—and, if necessary, disconnect from the UNIX computer.

Connecting to the UNIX Computer

If you turn on your terminal and see a message from the UNIX computer that looks something like this:

```
login:
```

you can probably skip ahead to the section, "Logging In." Otherwise, browse through the next few sections and find the one that applies to you. (We can't cover every user's situation exactly. If none of these suggestions help you enough, ask another UNIX user or your system administrator.)

Connecting from another operating system

If you're using a personal computer to connect to the UNIX system, you'll probably need to start a *terminal emulation* program. Some common programs are PROCOMM, QMODEM, KERMIT, and TELNET. (There are lots of others.)

If you start the program and get a UNIX login: prompt, you're ready to log in. But, if your screen stays blank or you get another message that you don't understand, check with another user or your system administrator for help.

Connecting with a data switch

Your office may have a data switch, a port contender, or another system that allows you to select which computer you will connect to. Like a telephone switchboard, this connects your terminal to one of a number of computers. Enter your computer's hostname or code number at the prompt—or choose from the menu of hosts.

Connecting from a window system

If you have an X terminal or a workstation, you should read the introductory sections of Chapter 2 to help you find the right steps for logging in.

Logging In

The process of making yourself known to the UNIX computer system and getting to your UNIX account is called *logging in*. Before you can start work, you must connect your terminal or window to the UNIX computer—then log in to UNIX and identify yourself. To log in, you enter your username (usually your name or initials) and a private password. The password does not appear on the screen as you enter it.

When you log in successfully, you will get some system messages and finally the UNIX shell prompt (where you can enter UNIX commands). A successful login to the system named *nutshell* would look something like this:

```
O'Reilly & Associates, Inc.
nutshell.ora.com: Solaris UNIX version 2.1

login: john
Password:
Last login: Wed Nov  3 14:34:51 EST 1993 from joe_pc
```

```
The hosts nutshell, mongo and cruncher will be down
for maintenance from 6 to 9 PM tonight.

Dyslexics of the world, untie!
Thu Nov  4 12:24:48 EST 1993
%
```

In this example, the system messages include a "fortune" and the date. Although this example doesn't show it, you may be asked for your *terminal type*, accounting or chargeback information, and so on. The last line to appear is the UNIX shell prompt. When you reach this point, you're logged in to your account and can start using UNIX commands.

The messages that appear when you log in differ from system to system and day to day. The shell prompt also differs. The examples in this book use the prompt "%".

Let's summarize logging in, step by step:

1. If needed, connect your terminal or window to the UNIX system.
2. If you don't have a login: prompt, press the $\boxed{\text{RETURN}}$ key a few times until you see that prompt on the screen.
3. Type in your username in *lowercase letters* at the prompt. For example, if your login name is "john," type:

    ```
    login: john
    ```

    Press the $\boxed{\text{RETURN}}$ key.

    The system should prompt you to enter your password. If passwords are not used on your system, you can skip the next step.
4. If you were assigned a password, type it at the prompt. For security, your password is not displayed on the screen as you type it:

    ```
    Password:
    ```

    Press the $\boxed{\text{RETURN}}$ key after you finish typing your password.

The system verifies your account name and password—and, if they are correct, logs you in to your account.

Problem Checklist

✓ *Nothing seemed to happen after I logged in.*

Wait for a minute, since the system may just be slow. If you still do not get anything, ask other users if they are having the same problem.

✓ *The system says "login incorrect".*

Try logging in again, taking care to enter the correct name and password. Be sure to type your username at the login: prompt and your password at the "password:" prompt. Backspacing may not work while entering either of these; if you make a mistake, use RETURN to get a new login: prompt and try again.

If you still fail after trying to log in a few more times, check with the System Administrator to make sure you are using the right username and password for your account.

✓ *All letters appear in* UPPERCASE *and may have backslashes* (\) *before them.*

You probably entered your username in uppercase. Type **exit** and log in again.

Remote Logins

The computer you log into may not be the computer you need to use. For instance, you might have a workstation on your desk but need to do some work on the main computer in another building. Or you might be a professor doing research with a computer at another university.

Your UNIX system can connect to other computers, then let you work as if you were sitting at the other computer. To do this, you first log in to your local computer. Then you start a program on your local computer that connects to the remote computer. Some typical programs are **telnet** and **rlogin** (for connecting over a computer network) as well as **cu** and **tip** (for connecting through telephone lines using a modem). You use the remote system until you're done; when you log off the remote computer, the remote-login program quits and returns you to your local computer.

The syntax for most remote-login programs is:

program-name *remote-hostname*

For example, if Dr. Nelson wanted to connect to the remote computer named *biolab.medu.edu*, she'd log in to her local computer first. Next, she'd use the **telnet** program to reach the remote computer. Her session might look something like this:

```
login: jennifer
Password:

NOTICE to all second-floor MDs: meeting in room 304 at 4 PM.
```

```
% telnet biolab.medu.edu

Medical University Biology Laboratory

biolab.medu.edu login: jdnelson
Password:

biolab%
     .
     .

     .
biolab% exit
Connection closed by foreign host.
%
```

Her account on the host *biolab* has a shell prompt with the hostname. This helps her tell that she's logged in remotely. If you use more than one system but don't have the hostname in your prompt, references in Appendix A (*UNIX Power Tools*, for example), will show you how.

The Nutshell Handbook *The Whole Internet User's Guide and Catalog* has more about **telnet** and **rlogin**. For more information about **cu** and **tip**, see the Nutshell Handbook, *Using uucp and Usenet.*

The UNIX Shell

Once you've logged in, you're working with a program called the *shell.* The shell interprets the commands you enter, runs the program you've asked for, and generally coordinates what happens between you and the UNIX operating system. There are three kinds of shells in common use: the Bourne, Korn, and C shell.

For a beginner, the differences between most shells are slight. However, you should ask your System Administrator which shell you are using. If you plan to do a lot of work in the UNIX environment, you will want to learn more about the shell and its set of special commands. Appendix A lists places to find more information.

The Shell Prompt

The shell prompt is the shell's way of saying that it is ready and waiting for you to enter a command. When the system is finished running a command, the shell replies with a prompt to tell you that you can now enter another command.

Bourne and Korn shell prompts usually contain a $. The C shell most often uses %. However, the prompt can be customized to give more information, so your own shell prompt may be different from what we show here.

Entering a Command

Entering a command at the UNIX shell prompt tells the computer what to do. Your command identifies a UNIX program by name. When you press the RETURN key, the shell interprets your command and executes the program.

The first word that you type at a shell prompt is always a UNIX command. Like most things in UNIX, command names are case-sensitive; if the command name is lowercase (and most are), you must type it in lowercase. Some simple commands consist of a single word.

date

One example of a single-word command is **date**. When you enter the command **date**, the current date and time are displayed on your screen.

```
% date
Thu Nov  4 13:39:24 EST 1993
```

When you are typing a command line, the system is simply collecting your input from the keyboard. Pressing the RETURN key tells the shell that you have finished entering text and that it can start executing the command.

who

Another simple command is **who**. It displays a list of the users that are currently logged in. The listing also shows you the number of the terminal they are using and the times that they logged in.

The **who** command can also tell you who is logged in at the terminal you are using. The command line is **who am i**. This command line consists of the command (**who**) and arguments (**am i**). (For an explanation of "arguments," see the section "Syntax of UNIX Commands" later in this chapter.)

```
% who am i
ruby!john     tty23    Nov  6 08:26       (diamond)
%
```

The response shown in this example says that:
- "I am" John.
- I'm logged on to the computer named "ruby."
- I'm using terminal 23.
- I logged in at 8:26 on the morning of November 6.
- I started my login from another computer named "diamond."

Not all versions of **who am i** give this much information.

Correcting a Mistake

What do you do if you make a mistake in typing a command? Suppose you typed in "dare" instead of "date" and pressed the RETURN key before you realized your mistake. The shell will give you an error message.

```
% dare
dare: command not found
%
```

Don't be too concerned about getting error messages. Sometimes it may even appear that you typed the command correctly, but you still get an error message. Sometimes this can be caused by typing control characters that are invisible on the screen. Once the prompt returns, re-enter your command.

If you notice a typing mistake before you press RETURN, you can backspace to erase the character and then enter the correct character.

The *erase character* differs from system to system and from account to account, and can be customized. The most common erase characters are:

- BACKSPACE
- DELETE, DEL, or RUBOUT key
- CTRL-H

CTRL-H is called a *control character*. To type a control character (for example, CTRL-H) hold down the CTRL key while typing the letter "h". (This is like the way you make an uppercase letter: hold the SHIFT key while typing a letter key.) In the text, we will write control characters as CTRL-H, but in the examples, we will use the standard notation: ^H. This is *not* the same as pressing the "^" (caret) key and then pressing the "h" key.

The key labeled DEL is often used as the *interrupt character* instead of the erase character. (It may be labeled DELETE or RUBOUT on some terminals.) This key is used to interrupt or cancel a command, and can be used anytime you want to quit what you are doing. Another character often programmed to do the same thing is CTRL-C.

Some other common control characters are:

CTRL-U   Erases the whole input line; you can start over.

CTRL-S   Pauses output from a program that is writing to the screen.

CTRL-Q   Restarts output after a pause by CTRL-S.

CTRL-D   Returns you to UNIX command level. Used to signal
          end-of-input for some programs (like **cat** and **mail**, see
          Chapter 3). May also log you out of the UNIX system.

Find the erase and interrupt characters for your account and write them
down:

_____   Backspace and erase a character

_____   Interrupt a command

In Chapter 3, we'll tell you how to change these characters if you like.

Logging Out

Logging out is the process of ending a UNIX session. You should *not* end a
session by just turning off your terminal! To log out, enter the command
exit. (In many cases, the command **logout** will also work.) Depending on
your shell, you may also be able to log out by pressing CTRL-D .

What happens next depends on the place you've logged in from:

• If your terminal is connected directly to the computer, the login: prompt
  should appear on the screen.

• If you are using a window system, the window will probably close. If
  you have additional windows open, you'll need to log out or close
  them, too. You may also need to shut off the window system itself.
  (See Chapter 2.)

• If you were connected to a remote computer, the system prompt from
  your local computer should reappear on your screen. (That is, you are
  still logged in to your local computer.) Repeat the process if you want
  to log out from the local computer.

After you've logged out, you can turn off your terminal or leave it on for the
next user.

Problem Checklist

In your first few sessions with UNIX, you are unlikely to experience any of
the following problems. However, these problems may occur later on, as
you begin to do more advanced work.

✓ *You get another shell prompt or the system says "logout: not login shell."*

You've been using a sub-shell (a shell created by your original login shell). To end each sub-shell, type **exit** (or just press CTRL-D) until you're logged out.

✓ *The system says, "There are stopped jobs."*

Many UNIX systems support a feature called *job control* that allows you to suspend programs temporarily while they are running. One or more of the programs you ran during your session has not ended, but is stopped (paused) instead. Enter **fg** to bring each stopped job into the foreground, then quit the program normally. (See Chapter 6.)

Syntax of UNIX Commands

UNIX commands can be simple, one-word entries like the **date** command. They can also be more complex: you may need to type more than the command name. Unfortunately, there's no standard way to write all UNIX commands.

A UNIX command may or may not have *arguments*. An argument can be an option or a filename. The general format for UNIX commands is:

command *option(s) filename(s)*

While there is no single set of rules for writing UNIX commands and arguments, you can use these general rules in most cases:

- Commands are entered in lowercase.
- *Options* modify the way in which a command works. Options are often single letters prefixed with a dash (–) and set off by any number of spaces or tabs.
- Multiple options in one command line can be set off individually. In some cases, you can combine them after a single dash.
- The argument *filename* is the name of a file that you want to use in some way. If you don't enter a filename correctly, you may get the response "*filename*: no such file or directory" or "*filename*: cannot open."
- You must type spaces between commands, option(s), and filename(s).
- Options come before filenames.
- Two or more commands can be written on the same line, each separated by a semicolon (;). Commands entered this way are executed one after another by the shell.

UNIX has a lot of commands! Don't try to memorize all of them. In fact, you'll probably need to know just a few commands and their options. As time goes on, you'll learn these commands and the best way to use them for your job. We cover some of the more useful UNIX commands in later chapters.

Let's look at an example of a UNIX command. The **ls** command displays a list of files. It can be used with or without arguments. If you enter:

```
% ls
```

a list of filenames will be displayed on the screen. But if you enter:

```
% ls -l
```

there will be an entire line of information for each file. The –l option (a dash and a lowercase letter "l") modifies the normal output of the **ls** command and lists files in the long format. You can also ask for information about a particular file by adding a filename as a second argument. For example, to find out about a file called *chap1*, you would enter:

```
% ls -l chap1
```

Many UNIX commands have more than one option. For instance, **ls** has a –a (*all*) option for listing hidden files. When you want to specify multiple options, you can write the command in one of the following equivalent forms:

```
% ls -a -l
% ls -al
```

You must type one space between the command name and the dash that introduces the options. If you enter **ls-al**, the shell will say "ls-al: command not found."

Exercise: Entering a few commands

There's no better way to become familiar with UNIX than by entering a few commands. To run a command, type in the command and then press the RETURN key. Remember that almost all UNIX commands are typed in lowercase.

Get today's date.	Enter **date**
List logged in users.	Enter **who**
Obtain more information about users.	Enter **who -u** or **finger** or **w**
Find out who is at your terminal.	Enter **who am i**

Enter two commands in the same line.	Enter **who am i;date**
Mistype a command.	Enter **woh**

In this session, you have practiced several simple commands and have seen the results on the screen.

Types of Commands

The section above was about UNIX commands: commands you enter at a shell prompt. Some UNIX commands have commands of their own. (For examples, look at the **more**, **mail**, and **pg** commands in Chapter 3. Text editors like **vi** and **emacs** also have their own commands.) Once you start the command, it prints its own prompt—and understands its own set of commands (not UNIX commands).

For instance, if you enter **mail**, you'll see a new prompt from the **mail** program. You'll enter mail commands to handle mail messages. When you enter the special command (q) to quit the **mail** program, **mail** will stop prompting you. Then you'll get another shell prompt; you can enter UNIX commands again.

The Unresponsive Terminal

During your UNIX session (while you're logged in), your terminal may not respond when you type a command, or the display on your screen may stop at an unusual place. That's called a "hung" or "frozen" terminal or session.

There are several reasons for a session to be hung. One of the most common is that the connection between your terminal and the computer gets too busy and your terminal has to wait its turn. (Other users or computers are probably sharing the same connection.) In that case, your session will start by itself in a few moments. You should *not* enter extra commands in an attempt to "un-hang" the session because those commands will all take effect after the connection resumes.

If the system doesn't respond for quite a while (and how long that is depends on your individual situation; ask your system administrator for advice), the following solutions will usually work. Try these in the order shown until the system responds.

1. Press the RETURN key.

   You may have typed a command but forgot to press RETURN to tell the shell that you are done typing and that it should interpret the command.

2. If you can type commands, but nothing happens when you press RETURN, try pressing LINE FEED or CTRL-J. If this works, your terminal needs to be reset to fix the RETURN key. Some systems have a **reset** command that you can run by typing CTRL-J reset CTRL-J. If this doesn't work, you may need to log out and log back in or turn your terminal off and on again.

3. If your shell has job control (see Chapter 6), press CTRL-Z.

   This suspends a program that may be running and gives you another shell prompt. Now you can enter the **jobs** command to find the program's name, then restart the program with **fg** or terminate it with **kill**.

4. Press your interrupt key (found earlier in this chapter—typically DELETE or CTRL-C).

   This interrupts a program that may be running. (Unless a program is run in the background, as described in Chapter 6, the shell will wait for it to finish before giving a new prompt. A long-running program may thus appear to hang the terminal.) If this doesn't work the first time, try it once more; doing it more than twice usually won't help.

5. Type CTRL-Q.

   If output has been stopped with CTRL-S, this will restart it. (Note that some programs will automatically issue CTRL-S if they need to pause output; this character may not have been typed from the keyboard.)

6. Check that the NO SCROLL key is not locked or toggled on.

   This key stops the screen display from scrolling upward. If your keyboard has a NO SCROLL key that can be toggled on and off by pressing it over and over, keep track of how many times you've pressed it as you try to free yourself. If it doesn't seem to help, be sure you've pressed it an even number of times; this leaves the key in the same state it was when you started.

7. Check the physical connections to the terminal and from the terminal to the system.

8. Type CTRL-D at the beginning of a new line.

   Some programs (like **mail**) expect text from the user. A program may be waiting for an end-of-input character from you to tell it that you've finished entering text. Typing CTRL-D may cause you to log out, so you should try this as a last resort.

9. If you're using a window system, close (terminate) the window you're using and open a new one. Otherwise, turn your terminal off, wait ten seconds or so, then turn it on again (this may also log you out).

If none of these work, ask a local system expert for help and watch carefully.

2

Using Window Systems

Introduction to Windowing

All versions of UNIX work with computer terminals that handle a single window, a single login session. Most modern UNIX versions support one or more *window systems*. A window system is a package of programs that let a terminal handle many sessions at once. Along with the keyboard, window systems use a *mouse* or another device (such as a trackball) to move a *pointer* across the screen. The pointer can select parts of the screen, move them, help you copy and paste text, work with menus of commands, and more. If you've used a Macintosh, Microsoft Windows, or OS/2 and its Presentation Manager (among others), you've used a window system. Figure 2-1 shows a typical display with windows.

This chapter introduces the X Window System (called X for short), the most common UNIX window system. This introduction should also help you use non-X window systems.

Like UNIX, X is very flexible. The appearance of windows, the way menus work, and more, are controlled by a program called the *window manager*. Three common window managers are **mwm** (Motif Window Manager), **olwm** (Open Look Window Manager), and **twm** (Tab Window Manager). There are plenty of other window managers. This chapter explains **mwm** and uses it in examples. The details of using other window managers, and the way they appear on the display, are somewhat different—but this chapter should help you use them, too.

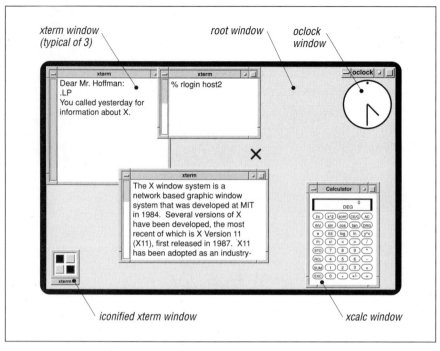

Figure 2-1: An X display with the mwm window manager

Starting X

There are several ways to start X and its window manager. This section explains a few of the most common ways. Figure 2-2 shows some steps along a few different paths to starting X. If your display is like any of the following, refer to the section noted. (If none of these fit your situation, skim through the next three sections or ask your system administrator for help.)

- Figure 2-2A, **xdm** is running. Start with Section A below.
- Figure 2-2B, you have a standard UNIX login session. Start with Section B.
- Figure 2-2C, X is running but a window manager probably isn't. (You can tell because the window doesn't have a "frame" around it.) Read Section C.
- Figure 2-2D, the window has a frame, so X and the **mwm** window manager are running. You can skip ahead to the next main section, "Running Programs."

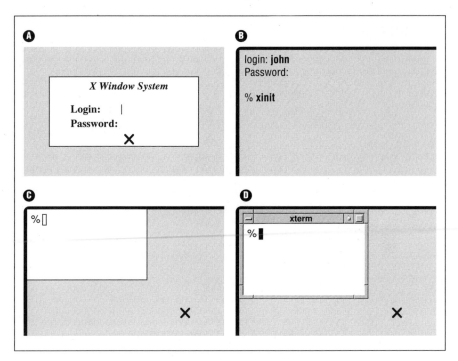

Figure 2-2: Some possibilities

A. Ready to Run X (with xdm)

Some terminals, like the one shown in Figure 2-2A, are ready to use X. When you start, there's a single window in the middle of the screen that says something like "X Window System on *hostname.*" The window has two other prompts, "Login:" and "Password:". A cursor (a vertical bar) sits to the right of the "Login:" line. Type your username (login name) and press RETURN. Do the same for your password. The login window disappears and a display something like Figure 2-1 appears.

You're ready to use X! Your terminal has probably been set up to use **xdm**, the X display manager; **xdm** logs you into your UNIX host and (usually) starts the window manager. You can skip ahead to the next main section, "Running Programs."

B. Starting X from a Standard UNIX session

If your terminal shows something like Figure 2-2B, with a standard UNIX login: prompt (not in a separate window; the whole screen looks like a terminal), then X is not running. Log in (as Chapter 1 explains) and get a shell prompt (like %). Next, you need to start X. The default command is:

```
% xinit
```

though your system may use another command instead. If all goes well, your screen will sprout at least one window. If the window looks like Figure 2-2C, without a frame from a window manager, read section C below. Otherwise, your window manager is running; skip ahead to the next main section, "Running Programs."

Problem Checklist

✓ *No windows open. I get the message "Fatal server error: No screens found."*

Your terminal may not be able to run X. Ask the system administrator.

C. Starting the Window Manager

Once you have a window open with a shell prompt in it (usually % or $), you can start the window manager program. Your account may have been set up to do this automatically. If a window manager is not running, windows won't have frames (with titles, control boxes, and so on). Also, if you move the pointer to the root window (sometimes called the "desktop") and press the mouse buttons, menus won't appear unless the window manager is running.

If you need to start the window manager, move your pointer into the window. Then enter this command at the shell prompt to start the Motif window manager:

```
% mwm &
[1] 12345
%
```

(To start **twm**, **olwm**, or another window manager, the command you'd type would be the name of that window manager.) In a few moments, the window should have a frame. (For more about starting programs, refer to "The xterm Window" section, below.)

Running Programs

One of the most important X features is that windows can come either from programs running on another computer or from an operating system other than UNIX. So, if your favorite MS/DOS program doesn't run under UNIX but has an X interface, you can run the program under MS/DOS and display its windows with X on your UNIX computer. Researchers can run graphical data analysis programs on supercomputers in other parts of the country and see the results in their offices. There's much more than we could cover here. The O'Reilly & Associates book *X Window System User's Guide, Volume Three, OSF/Motif 1.2 Edition* has all the details.

Setting Focus

Of all the windows on your screen, only one window receives the keystrokes you type. This window is usually highlighted in some way. By default in the **mwm** window manager, for instance, the frame of the window that receives your input is a darker shade of grey. In X jargon, choosing the window you type to is called "setting the *input focus.*" Most window managers can be configured to set the focus in one of the following two ways:

- Point to the window and click a mouse button (usually the first button). You may need to click on the title bar at the top of the window.
- Simply move the pointer inside the window.

When you use **mwm**, any new windows will get the input focus automatically as they pop up.

The xterm Window

One of the most important windows is an **xterm** window. **xterm** makes a terminal emulator window with a UNIX login session inside, just like a miniature terminal. You can have several **xterm** windows at once, each doing something different. To enter a UNIX command or answer a prompt in a window, set the focus there and type. Programs in other windows will keep running; if they need input from you, they'll wait just as they would on a separate terminal.

Figure 2-2D and Figure 2-4 (page 24) show a single **xterm** window with a shell prompt (%) inside. If you enter a UNIX command (like **date**), it will run just as it would on a non-window terminal.

You can also start separate X-based window programs (typically called *clients*) by entering commands in an **xterm** window. Although you can start new clients (**xterm**, **xcalc**, and so on) from any open **xterm** window on your computer, we recommend starting all of them from the first window that you opened. If you do that, and if your shell has job control (Chapter 6), it's easy to find and control all the clients.

Here's an example. To start the calculator called **xcalc**, enter:

```
% xcalc &
[1] 12345
%
```

The shell will print a PID number like 12345. (Chapter 6 has more information.) If you forget to type the ampersand (&) at the end of the line, kill (terminate) **xcalc** with your interrupt character (like CTRL-C) to get another shell prompt—then enter the command correctly.

The new window may be placed and get the focus automatically. Or, the window (or an outline of it) may "float" above the display, following the pointer—until you point somewhere and click the mouse button to place the window.

You can also start a new **xterm** from an existing **xterm**. Just enter **xterm &** (don't forget the ampersand) at the shell prompt.

The same method works for starting other X programs.

The Root Menu

If you move the pointer onto the root window (the "desktop" behind the windows) and press the correct mouse button (usually the first or third button, depending on your setup), you should see the *root menu*. You may need to hold down the button to keep the menu visible. The root menu has commands for controlling windows. The menu's commands may differ depending on the system.

Your system administrator (or you, if you study your window manager) can add commands to the root menu. These can be window manager operations or commands to open other windows. For example, a "New Window" menu item can open a new **xterm** window for you. A "Calculator" item could start **xcalc**.

Exercise

Change to your home directory.	Enter **cd**
Open two **xterm** windows.	Enter **xterm &** twice or select that item twice on the root menu.
Practice setting focus on both new windows and entering UNIX commands in each.	Click on window and/or move pointer there. Enter **who am i**, etc.
Start the clock from one window.	Enter **oclock &**
Start the calculator from one window and try it.	Enter **xcalc &**
Change working directory in only *one* window.	Enter **cd /bin**
Check working directory in *both* windows.	Enter **pwd**
Terminate **xcalc**.	Set focus on the **xcalc**, type your interrupt character (like CTRL-C).

Problem Checklist

✓ *When I try to start a client, I see "connection refused by server" or "client is not authorized to connect to server."*

You may need to run the **xhost** command. See your system administrator or an experienced X user.

✓ *When I try to start a client, I see "Error: Can't open display."*

Your DISPLAY environment variable may not be set correctly or you may need to use the *–display* option. Ask for help or refer to the *X User's Guide.*

Working with a Mouse

Let's look at some basics of using a mouse or other pointing devices.

Pointer Shape

As you move the mouse pointer* from the root window onto other windows or menus, the shape of the pointer will change. For instance, on the

---

*The correct word for this symbol is *cursor.* But **xterm** and some other windows also have separate cursors to show where text will be entered. To avoid confusion, we use the word "pointer" for the cursor that moves all across the display under control of the mouse.

root window, the pointer is a big X. The pointer may change to an hour glass shape to tell you to wait. When you resize a window, the pointer changes to a cross with arrows.

Pointing, Clicking, Dragging

What's "pointing and clicking"? That's when you move the pointer to a place (usually over part of a window), then quickly press and release a mouse button (usually the first button). It's the same idea as pressing a button on a telephone or another electronic appliance.

Something else you'll do is "dragging." That means moving the pointer to a place (such as the corner of a window), then pressing a mouse button and holding it down while you move the pointer. This is called "dragging" a pointer or object, because the object will be dragged along with the pointer until you let go of the mouse button.

Using a Mouse with xterm Windows

Xterm windows have an advantage over plain UNIX terminals in that you can copy and paste text within a window or between windows. To get started, move the pointer inside an **xterm** window and select the window (set the focus there). Notice that the pointer changes to an "I-beam" shape. There's also a block cursor. As you type, notice that text you input appears at the block-shaped cursor, just like it would on a standard terminal. So, think of the block cursor as the window's input point.

The I-beam pointer selects text for copying. Let's try it. Point to the first character of a command line (not the prompt) and click the first mouse button. Next, move the pointer to the end of the text you want to select and click the third button. The text between the first and third clicks should be highlighted. (If you accidentally click another button, you may need to start over again.) Your **xterm** window should look something like Figure 2-3.

Next, click (don't hold) the second (middle) mouse button. The selected text will be copied into the window at the block cursor, just as if you typed it in. Press RETURN to run the command line; otherwise, backspace over it to get back to the prompt.

You can also select text by clicking in an **xterm** window. Point to a word and double-click (click twice, quickly) the first button; the word should be highlighted. Point to a line and triple-click to highlight the whole line. You can select and copy any text, not just command lines.

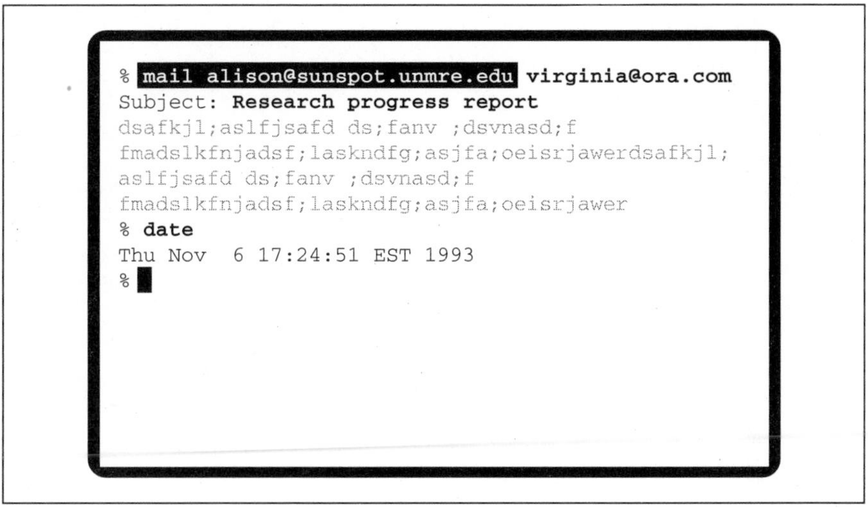

```
% mail alison@sunspot.unmre.edu virginia@ora.com
Subject: Research progress report
dsafkjl;aslfjsafd ds;fanv ;dsvnasd;f
fmadslkfnjadsf;laskndfg;asjfa;oeisrjawerdsafkjl;
aslfjsafd ds;fanv ;dsvnasd;f
fmadslkfnjadsf;laskndfg;asjfa;oeisrjawer
% date
Thu Nov  6 17:24:51 EST 1993
% █
```

Figure 2-3: Copying and pasting a command Line

The same copying and pasting works between **xterm** windows and between many other (but not all) windows that handle text. You can select text in one window and paste it into the other window. This is very handy for text editing.

Working with Windows

A window manager program helps you control windows. This section explains how **mwm** manages windows. Other window managers do the same kinds of things—but with some variation. Let's start by looking at Figure 2-4, a typical window under **mwm**.

The top part of every window has a *titlebar* with the title of the window and three buttons. The edges of the window can be used to resize the window. (See the NOTE in the section below called "Resizing Windows.")

Using the Titlebar

The top part of a window has three buttons (see Figure 2-4).

The two buttons at the top right corner have boxes inside them. Clicking the button with the small box makes the window as small as possible; the window turns into an *icon*. "Iconifying" puts unneeded windows out of the way without quitting the program inside them; it also keeps you from accidentally typing into a window. (Figure 2-1 shows an icon.) The button with the big square *maximizes* a window. That makes it as big as the client will allow, often as big as the screen.

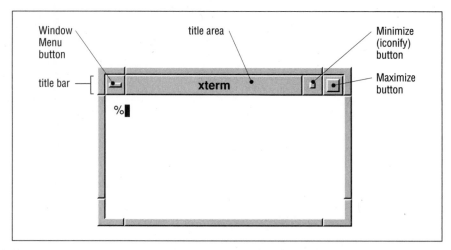

Figure 2-4: A window running with the Motif Window Manager

The left-hand button opens the window menu; this is explained in "The Window Menu" section, below.

Moving Windows and Icons

To move a window, start by pointing to the titlebar. To move an icon, point to it. Hold down the first mouse button and drag to the new location—then let go of the button. You can also start the move from the window menu (see below) but we think this way is easier.

Resizing Windows

If you have the pointer inside a window and then move the pointer to an edge, the pointer will change to an arrow shape. The arrow points the direction that you can resize the window. If you pointed to one of the corners, you can resize both sides that meet at the corner. To resize when you have the arrow pointer, press and hold the first button—then drag the window border until the window size is what you want and release the button. If you don't get quite the size you want, just do it again.

NOTE

On some versions of UNIX and with some programs, changing the size of an **xterm** window may confuse programs run in that window. Also, remember that many UNIX terminals are 80 characters wide; if you're editing text in a window and change its width to something besides 80 characters, that can cause trouble later when people read the file on a standard 80 character-wide terminal.

The Window Menu

Under **mwm**, each window can be controlled by its own *window menu*. There are lots of ways to get a window menu. Here are two: when you click on the menu button at the top-left corner of a frame (Figure 2-4), and when you click on an icon. Figure 2-5 shows a window menu.

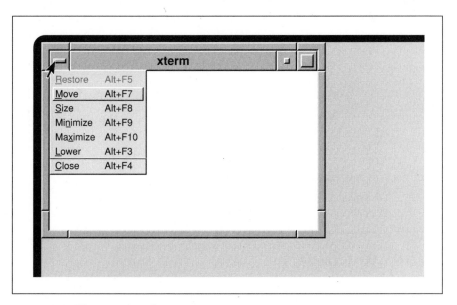

Figure 2-5: The mwm window menu

When the menu pops up, you can point to one of the items and click on it:

- **Restore** restores a minimized (icon) or maximized window to its original size. In Figure 2-5, the **Restore** entry is in a lighter typeface; this means you can't select it. (The window is already its normal size; restoring it wouldn't do anything.)
- **Move** lets you reposition a window on the screen.

- **Resize** lets you change a window's size. (See the preceding NOTE.)
- **Minimize** and **Maximize** operations were explained in "Using the Titlebar."
- **Lower** moves a window to the bottom of the stack, if it's in a stack of windows.
- **Close** terminates the window and the program in it. Use this as a "last resort." If the program has a separate menu or quit command (for example, entering **exit** at a shell prompt in an **xterm** window), use it instead of using **Close**. (See the section *Quitting* below, for explanation.)

On the menu, a *keyboard shortcut* follows each command. You don't have to use the mouse to choose commands. For example, to **Minimize** (iconify) a window, hold down the ALT (or META) key and press the F9 key. The shortcut for bringing up the window menu (and taking it away) is to hold the SHIFT key and press the ESC (ESCAPE) key. If your keyboard doesn't have all of those keys, the menu can be customized to use different keys. Our *X Window System User's Guide* explains how.

Exercise

Copy and paste part of a command line.	Type **who am i;date** and press RETURN in one **xterm** window. Highlight the **who am i**, set focus to the other **xterm** window, and copy the command there.
Move a window.	Grab and drag the window by its titlebar.
Iconify a window from the titlebar.	Use the Mimimize button.
Restore the icon.	Select **Restore** from the window menu.

Other X Clients

Here are a few of the X client programs that your system may have:

- **resize**: helps programs in **xterm** windows recognize new window size
- **xbiff**: tells you when new electronic mail comes in
- **xclipboard**: helps with copying and pasting text
- **xdpr**: prints a window (with the printer)
- **xedit**: simple text editor
- **xmag**: magnifies parts of the screen
- **xman**: browses UNIX manual (reference) pages

- **xmh**: electronic mail program
- **xset**: sets user preferences

For more information on those programs, see your online documentation or our *X Window System User's Guide.*

Quitting

Like almost everything in X, the way to quit X is configurable. The key to shutting down X is to know which one of your programs (your windows or window manager) is the *controlling program.* When the controlling program quits, any other leftover X programs are killed immediately. The controlling program is usually either the window manager or the single **xterm** window that started your X session.

Find the controlling program for your X session and write it down:

_____ Program to quit last

If your controlling program is an **xterm** window, we suggest leaving that window iconified from just after you've logged in until you've shut down all the other X clients. That way, you won't end your X session accidentally by ending that **xterm** window too soon.

To quit the window manager, select the **Exit** or **Quit** command on the root menu.

Here are the steps to shut down X:

1. Quit all non-controlling programs (all programs *other* than the controlling program):

    If any windows are running programs that have their own "quit" commands, it's a good idea to use those special commands to quit. For example, if you're running a text editor in an **xterm** window, use the editor's "quit" command, then finish the **xterm** window by entering **exit** at the shell prompt.

    Using the program's own "quit" command gives the program time to clean up and shut down gracefully. On the other hand, the **Close** item on the **mwm** window menu can interrupt and kill a program before it's ready. If, however, a program doesn't have its own "quit" command, use **Close** on the window menu.

    If any icons are running programs that have their own "quit" command, open the icons into windows and use the "quit" commands.

2. Quit the controlling program.

   After X shuts down, you may get a UNIX shell prompt. If you do, you can log out by entering **exit**. If you simply get another login box from **xdm** (as in Figure 2-2A), you're done.

3

Your UNIX Account

Once you log in, you can use the many facilities UNIX provides. You, as an authorized user of the system, will have an account that will provide:

- A place in the UNIX filesystem where you can store your files.
- A username that identifies you, lets you control access to your files and receive messages from other users.
- A customizable environment that you can tailor to your liking.

The UNIX Filesystem

A *file* is the unit of storage in UNIX, as in many other systems. A file can contain anything: text (a report you're writing, a to-do list), a program, digitally encoded pictures or sound, and so on—all are just sequences of raw data until they are interpreted by the right program.

In UNIX, files are organized into directories. A *directory* is actually a special kind of file where the system stores information about other files. A directory can be thought of as a place, so that files are said to be contained *in* directories and you are said to work *inside* a directory. (If you have used a Macintosh computer, a UNIX directory is a lot like a Macintosh folder. Directories under MS/DOS and UNIX are almost identical.)

Your Home Directory

When you log in to UNIX, you are placed in a directory called your *home directory*. This home directory, a unique place in the UNIX filesystem, contains the files you use almost every time you log in. In your home directory, you can create your own files. As you'll see in a minute, you can also store your own directories within your home directory. Like folders in a file cabinet, this is a good way to organize your files.

Your Working Directory

Your *current working directory* (often called your working directory) is the directory you are currently working in. At the start of every session, your home directory is your working directory. You may change to another directory, in which case the directory you moved to becomes your working directory.

Unless you tell UNIX otherwise, all commands that you enter apply to the files in your working directory. In the same way, when you create files, they are created in your working directory.

The Directory Tree

The directories are organized into a hierarchical structure that is usually imagined as a family tree. The parent directory of the tree is known as the *root directory* and is written as a slash (/).

The root contains several directories. Figure 3-1 shows the top of an imaginary UNIX filesystem tree—the root directory and some of the directories under the root.

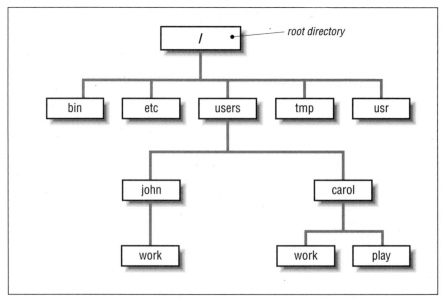

Figure 3-1: Example of a directory tree

bin, etc, users, tmp, and *usr* are some of the *subdirectories* (child directories) of *root.* These are fairly standard directories and usually contain specific kinds of system files. For instance, *bin* contains many UNIX commands. Not all systems have a directory named *users*; it may be called *u, home,* and/or be located in some other part of the filesystem.

In our example, the directory *users* has a parent directory *root* that is one level above. It also has two subdirectories, *john* and *carol,* that are one level below. On a UNIX system, each directory has one parent directory* and may have one or more subdirectories. The subdirectories (like *carol*) may have subdirectories themselves (like *work* and *play*), to a limitless depth for practical purposes.

The notation used to specify file and directory locations is called a *pathname.* A pathname is like an address and locates the directory or file in the UNIX filesystem. We'll look at pathnames in a moment.

On a basic UNIX system, all files in the filesystem are stored on disks connected to your computer. It isn't always easy to use the files on someone else's computer or for someone on another computer to use your files. Your system may have an easier way: a *networked filesystem* with a name like *NFS* or *RFS.* Networked filesystems make a remote computer's files appear as if they're part of your computer's directory tree. For instance, your computer in Phoenix might have a directory named *boston.* When you look in that subdirectory, you'll see some (or all) of the directory tree from your company's computer in Boston. Your system administrator can tell you if your computer has any networked filesystems.

Absolute Pathnames

The UNIX filesystem organizes its files and directories in an inverted tree structure with the root directory at the top. An *absolute pathname* tells you the path of directories you must travel to get from the root to the directory or file you want. In a pathname, put slashes (/) between the directory names.

For example, */users/john* is an absolute pathname and defines a unique directory as follows:
- the root is the first "/"

---

*Q: Which directory doesn't seem to have a parent directory? A: On most UNIX systems, the *root* directory, at the top of the tree, is *its own* parent. Some systems have another directory above the root.

- the directory *users* (a subdirectory of *root*)
- the directory *john* (a subdirectory of *users*)

Be sure not to type spaces anywhere in the pathname. This structure is shown in Figure 3-2 below.

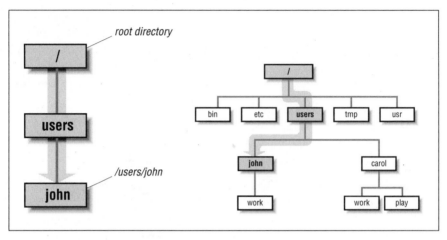

Figure 3-2: Absolute path of directory john

If you look at Figure 3-2, you'll see that the directory *john* has a subdirectory named *work*. Its absolute pathname is */users/john/work*.

The root is always indicated by the slash (/) at the start of the pathname.

Relative Pathnames

Another way of writing the address of a file or directory is to use a *relative pathname*. A relative pathname gives the location relative to your working directory.

Unless you specify an absolute pathname (starting with a slash), UNIX assumes that you're using a relative pathname. Like absolute pathnames, relative pathnames can go through more than one directory level by naming the directories along the path.

For example, if you're currently in the *users* directory (see Figure 3-2), the relative pathname to the *carol* directory below is simply *carol*. The relative pathname to the *play* directory below that is *carol/play*.

Notice that neither of the pathnames in the previous example starts with a slash. That's what makes them relative pathnames! Those pathnames start at the working directory, not the root directory.

Exercise

Here's a short but important exercise. The example above explained the relative pathname *carol/play*. What do you think UNIX would say about the pathname */carol/play*? (Look again at Figure 3-2.)

UNIX would say "No such file or directory." Why? (Please think about that before you read more. It's very important and it's one of the most common beginner's mistakes.) Here's the answer. The pathname */carol/play* is an absolute pathname starting from the root: it says to look in the *root* directory for a subdirectory named *carol*. But there is no subdirectory named *carol* one level directly below the root, so the pathname is wrong. The only absolute pathname to the *play* directory is */users/carol/play*.

Relative pathnames up

You can go up the tree by using the shorthand ".." (dot dot) for the parent directory. You can also go down the tree by specifying directory names. You just name each step along the way, separated by a slash (/).

Figure 3-3 shows a part of Figure 3-1. If your working directory in the figure is *work*, there are two pathnames for the *play* subdirectory of *carol*. You already know how to write the absolute pathname, */users/carol/play*. Alternatively, you can go up one level (using the ".." notation) to *carol*, then go down the tree to *play*. Figure 3-3 shows that.

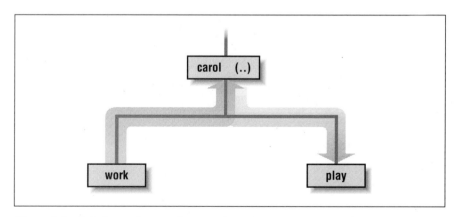

Figure 3-3: Relative pathname from work to play

The relative pathname would be *../play*. It would be wrong to give the relative address as *carol/play*. Using *carol/play* would say that *carol* is a subdirectory of your working directory instead of what it is in this case: the parent directory.

Absolute and relative pathnames are totally interchangeable. UNIX commands simply follow whatever path you specify to wherever it leads. If you use an absolute pathname, the path starts from the root. If you use a relative pathname, the path starts from your working directory. Choose whichever is easier at the moment.

Changing Your Working Directory

When you know the absolute or relative pathname of a file or directory, you can move up and down the UNIX directory tree.

pwd

To find out what directory you are currently in, use the **pwd** (print working directory) command. The **pwd** command takes no arguments.

```
% pwd
/users/john
%
```

pwd prints the absolute pathname of your working directory.

cd

You can change your working directory to any directory (or to another user's directory—if you have permission) with the **cd** (change directory) command.

The **cd** command has the form:

> **cd** *pathname*

The argument pathname can be an absolute or a relative pathname for the directory you want to change to. Use the form that is most convenient for you at the time.

```
% cd /users/carol
% pwd
/users/carol
% cd work
% pwd
/users/carol/work
%
```

The command **cd**, with no arguments, will always take you back to your home directory from wherever you are in the filesystem.

Note that you can only change to another directory. You cannot **cd** to a filename. If you try, UNIX will give you an error message:

```
% cd /etc/passwd
/etc/passwd:  Not a directory
%
```

/etc/passwd is a file that contains information about users allowed to log in to the system.

Files in the Directory Tree

A directory can hold directories. And, of course, a directory can hold files. Figure 3-4 is a close-up of the filesystem around *john*'s home directory. The four files are shown along with the *work* subdirectory.

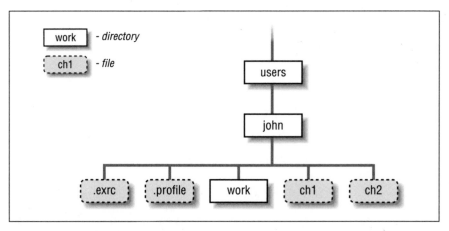

Figure 3-4: Files in the directory tree

Pathnames to files are made the same way as pathnames to directories. For example, if your working directory is *users*, the relative pathname to the *work* directory below would be *john/work*. The relative pathname to the *ch1* file would be *john/ch1*.

Listing Files

To use the **cd** command, you must decide which entries in a directory are subdirectories and which are files. The **ls** command is used to list the entries in the directory tree.

ls

When you enter the **ls** command, you will get a listing of the files and subdirectories contained in your working directory. The syntax is simple:

ls *option(s) directory-and-filename(s)*

If you've just logged in for the first time, entering **ls** without any arguments may seem to do nothing. This is not surprising, since you have not yet created any files in your working directory. If you have no files, nothing is displayed and you will simply get a new shell prompt.

```
% ls
%
```

But if you have previously created some files in your account, those filenames are displayed. The output you get will depend on the files you have in the directory. The display should look something like this:

```
% ls
ch1     ch10    ch2     ch3     intro
%
```

(Many System V systems display filenames in a single column. If yours does, you can change the display to columns with the *–x* option.) There are quite a few options that make **ls** show different amounts of information and change the format of the display.

The *–a* option (for *all*) is guaranteed to show you some more files, as in the following example:

```
% ls -a
.       .exrc     ch1     ch2     intro
..      .profile  ch10    ch3
%
```

At least two new files have appeared, with the names "." (dot) and ".." (dot dot). As mentioned earlier, .. is a special notation for the parent directory. A single . is a special notation for the working directory. There may also be other files, like *.profile* or *.exrc*. Any file whose name begins with a dot is hidden—it will be listed only if you use **ls -a**. (The file *.profile* contains commands that are automatically executed by the Bourne or Korn shells whenever you log in. The C shell uses the two files *.login* and *.cshrc* instead of *.profile*. The *.exrc* file contains commands that are automatically executed by the *ex* or *vi* editors when you start either one.)

To get more information about each file, add the *–l* option. (That's a lower-case letter "L" for *long*.) This option can be used alone, or in combination with *–a*, as shown in Figure 3-5.

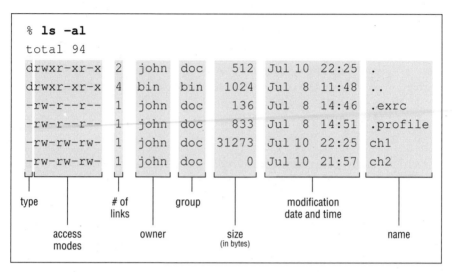

Figure 3-5: Output from ls -al

The long format provides the following information about each file:

Total *n*	*n* amount of storage used by the files in this directory.
Type	Tells whether the file is a directory (*d*) or a plain file (–). (There are other less common types that we don't explain here.)
Access modes	Specifies three types of users (yourself, your group, all others) who are allowed to read (*r*), write (*w*), or execute (*x*) your files.
Links	The number of files and directories linked to the file.
Owner	Who created or owns the file.
Group	The group that owns the file (if your version of UNIX doesn't show this column, add the *–g* option to see it).
Size (in bytes)	The size of the file.
Modification date	When the file was last modified.
Name	Name of the file or directory.

Notice especially the columns that list the owner and group of the files, and the access modes (also called permissions). The person who creates a file is its owner; if you've created any files (or the system administrator did it for you), this column should show your username. You also belong to a group, to which you were assigned by the system administrator. Files you create will either be marked with the name of your group or, in some cases, the group that owns the directory.

The *permissions* control who can read, write (modify) or execute the file (if it is a program). There are a total of ten characters in the permissions listing. The first character shows the file type (directory or plain file). The next three characters show the permissions for the file's owner—you if you created the file. The next three characters show permissions for other members of the file's group. The final three characters show permissions for all other users.

For example, the permissions for *.profile* are -rw-r--r--. So it is a plain file. You, the owner, have both read and write permissions. But other users of the system can only read the file; they cannot modify the file.

In the case of directories, **x** means the permission to access the directory—for example, to run a command that reads a file there or to use a subdirectory. Notice that the two directories shown in the example are executable (searchable by you, by your group, and by everyone else on the system). A directory with **w** (write) permission allows deleting, renaming, or adding files within the directory. Read (**r**) permission allows listing the directory with **ls**.

You can use the **chmod** command to change the permissions of your files and directories. See the section of this chapter called "Protecting and Sharing Files."

If you are only interested in knowing which files are directories and which are executable files, you can use the *–F* (uppercase "F") option. If you give the pathname to a directory, **ls** will list the directory but it will *not* change your working directory. The **pwd** command in the following example shows that.

```
% ls -F /users/andy
calendar    goals    ideas/
ch2         guide/   testpgm*
% pwd
/etc
%
```

ls -F lists each directory with a / (slash) at the end of its name. In our example, *guide* and *ideas* are directories. You can verify this by listing the files with the *−l* option and noting the "d" in the first field of the output. Files with an execute status (**x**), like programs, are marked with an * (asterisk). The file *testpgm* is an executable file. Files that are not marked are not executable.

Exercise: Exploring the filesystem

You are now equipped to explore the filesystem with **cd**, **ls**, and **pwd**. Try a few **cd** commands interspersed with **pwd** commands. Take a tour of the directory system, hopping many steps at a time.

Go to your home directory.	Enter **cd**
Find your working directory.	Enter **pwd**
Change to new working directory.	Enter **cd /etc**
List files in new working directory.	Enter **ls**
Change directory to root and list files.	Enter **cd /; ls**
Change to a new directory.	Enter **cd usr**
Give a wrong pathname.	Enter **cd xqk**
Change to a new directory with its absolute pathname.	Enter **cd /etc**
List files in another directory.	Enter **ls /bin**
Find your working directory (notice that ls didn't change it).	Enter **pwd**
Return to your home directory.	Enter **cd**

Looking Inside Files

By now, you're probably tired of looking at files from the outside. It's kind of like going to a bookstore and looking at the covers, but never getting to read a word. Let's look at three programs for reading files: the **cat**, **more**, and **pg** commands.

cat

Most first-time users of UNIX think that *cat* is a strange name for a program. As we'll see later, *cat*, which is actually short for "concatenate," is used to put files together (to concatenate them) in order to create a bigger file. It can also be used to display files on your screen.

To display files on the standard output (your screen; see Chapter 5), use:

cat *file(s)*

For example, let's display the contents of the file */etc/passwd.* This file, which contains the names of users who have accounts, is used by the system each time you log in. (Your computer may have a more complete list somewhere else.)

```
% cat /etc/passwd
root:x&k8KP30f;(:0:0:Root:/:
daemon:*:1:1:Admin:/:
    .
    .
    .
%
```

cat works best for short files containing one screenful or less. If you **cat** a file that is too long, it may roll up the screen faster than you can read it. You cannot go back to view the previous screens when you use **cat**.

If you enter **cat** without a filename, press CTRL-D once to get out.

more

If you want to "read" a long file on the screen, your system may have the **more** command to display one screen or "page" of text at a time. A standard terminal screen can usually display 24 lines of text; a window can display any number of lines. The syntax is:

more *file(s)*

more allows you to move forward in the files by any number of pages or lines. Most versions let you move backward, too. You can also move back and forth between two or more files specified on the command line. When you invoke **more**, the first "page" of the file appears on the screen. A prompt appears at the bottom of the screen, as in the following example:

```
% more ch03
A file is the unit of storage in UNIX as in many other systems.
A file can be anything:  a program,
    .
    .
    .
--More--(47%)
```

The prompt says that you are 47% of your way through the file. The cursor sits to the right of this prompt as a signal for you to enter a **more** command to tell **more** what to do.

You can enter "h" (for "help") at the **more** prompt to display the **more** commands available on your system. Some of the simpler, but quite useful ones are given in Table 3-1 below.

Table 3-1: Useful more Commands

Command	Description
SPACE	Display next page.
RETURN	Display next line.
*n*f	Move forward *n* pages.
b	Move backward one page.
*n*b	Move backward *n* pages.
/*word*	Search forward for *word*.
?*word*	Search backward for *word*.
v	Start the **vi** editor at this point.
CTRL-L	Redisplay current page.
h	Help.
:n	Go to next file on command line.
:p	Go back to previous file on command line.
q	Quit **more** before end of file.

pg

The **more** command is not available on some UNIX systems. Most other systems have the **pg** command instead. It works like **more** but has different features. For example, **pg** lets you move to specific lines.

The format of the command is:

    pg *filename(s)*

If your system has **pg**, try it on a file that has more lines than your screen. Your screen displays the first page of the file. The last line is a colon (:) prompt. Press RETURN to view the next page or enter "q" to quit. Enter "h" to see what commands are available with **pg**.

Protecting and Sharing Files

UNIX makes it easy for users to share files and directories. Controlling exactly who has access takes some explaining, though—more explaining that we can do here. So here's a cookbook set of instructions. If you have critical security needs or you just want more information, see the references in Appendix A.

Directory Access Permissions

A directory's access permissions help to control access to the files in it. They affect ability to use all the files in the directory. (The ability to read or modify individual files in the directory is controlled by the file access permissions; see the second list below.)

In the commands below, replace *dirname* with the directory's pathname. An easy way to change permissions on the current directory is by using its relative pathname, . (dot), as in "**chmod 555 .**".

- To keep yourself from accidentally removing files (or adding or renaming files) in a directory, use **chmod 555** *dirname*. To do the same, but also deny other users any access, use **chmod 500** *dirname*.
- To protect the files in a directory and all its subdirectories from everyone else on your system—but be able to do anything *you* want to there—use **chmod 700** *dirname*.
- To let other people on the system see what's in a directory—and read or edit the files if the file permissions let them—but not rename, remove or add files—use **chmod 755** *dirname*.
- To let people in your UNIX group add, delete, and rename files in a directory of yours—and read or edit other people's files if the file permissions let them—use **chmod 775** *dirname*.
- To give full access to everyone on the system, use **chmod 777** *dirname*.

Remember, to access a directory, a user must also have execute (**x**) permission to all of its parent directories, all the way up to the root.

File Access Permissions

The access permissions on a file control what can be done to the file's *contents*. The access permissions on the *directory* where the file is kept control whether the file can be renamed or removed:

- To make a private file that only you can edit, use **chmod 600** *filename*. To protect it from accidental editing, use **chmod 400** *filename*.

- To edit a file yourself, and let everyone else on the system read it without editing, use **chmod 644** *filename.*
- To let you and all members of your UNIX group edit a file—but keep any other user from reading or editing it—use **chmod 660** *filename.* To let non-group users read but not edit the file, use **chmod 664** *filename.*
- To let anyone read or edit the file, use **chmod 666** *filename.*

Problem Checklist

✓ *I get the message "chmod: Not owner."*

Only the owner of a file or directory can set its permissions. Use **ls -l** to find the owner.

Electronic Mail

When you log in to your system, you may see a notice that says "You have mail." Someone has sent you a message or document by *electronic mail* (e-mail). With e-mail, you can compose a message at your terminal and send it to another user or list of users. You can also read any messages that others may have sent to you.

E-mail has several advantages over paper mail: it is convenient if you are already logged in, it is delivered much more quickly, it can be sent to any number of people almost as easily as to just one person, and both you and the recipient can store messages in the filesystem for reference.

There are a lot of e-mail programs for UNIX. Some UNIX systems have only an old, simple-minded program named *mail*, which this book doesn't cover. Most UNIX systems have a Berkeley program called *Mail* (with an uppercase "M"), *mailx*, or just *mail*. A similar but more powerful mail program is called *mush*. The basic commands in these latter programs are similar.

Sending Mail

Your mail's recipient doesn't have to be logged in. The messages you send are stored in the recipient's "mailbox," a file deep in the UNIX filesystem (often located in the directory */usr/mail*). Messages are kept there until the recipient logs in and decides to read them.

To send mail, give the address of the person(s) to whom you want to send a message, as in the following:

mail *address1 address2* ...

There are several kinds of addresses, too many to explain here. If you have questions, see one of the references in Appendix A or ask your system administrator or postmaster (the person who maintains your e-mail system). The most common addresses have this syntax:

username@hostname

username is the person's username and *hostname* is the name of their computer. If the recipient reads e-mail on the same computer you do, you may omit the *@hostname*. To keep a copy of your message, just add your username to the list of addresses.

After you enter **mail** and the addresses, the program will prompt you for the subject of the message. Type a one-line summary of the message (just like a paper memo) and press RETURN. Type in your message, line by line, pressing the RETURN key after every line, just as you would on a typewriter. When you have finished entering text, type CTRL-D on a separate line. You should get the shell prompt at this point. You can cancel a message while you are still entering text by entering ~q (a tilde character, then the letter "q") at the start of a line. The cancelled message is placed in a file called *dead.letter* in your home directory. To see other commands you can use while sending mail, enter ~? (tilde question mark) at the start of a line of your message, then press RETURN. To redisplay your message after using ~?, enter ~p at the start of a line.

```
% mail alicia@moxco.chi.il.us
Subject: My trip to Chicago is on!
Alicia, my travel request for your meeting was
approved.  Please send me the agenda.  Thanks.
^D
%
```

If you change your mind about Alicia's meeting, you will have to send her another message since you cannot cancel a message after you have pressed CTRL-D.

Reading Your Mail

To read your mail, simply enter **mail** (or the name of your system's e-mail command) at the shell prompt. You can do this any time during the UNIX session, not just when you log in.

Let's read Jerry's message to Alicia:

```
% mail
Mail version SMI 4.0 Wed Oct 23 10:38:28 PDT 1991  Type ? for help.
"/usr/spool/mail/alicia": 2 messages 1 new
>U  1 bigboss            Sat May 22 06:56   19/529  In your spare time
 N  2 jerry@syracuse.ed  Thu Nov  4 14:25   14/362  My trip to Chicago
& 2
Message  2:
Date: Thu, 4 Nov 1993 14:25:43 EST
From: jerry@syracuse.edu (Jerry Peek)
To: alicia@moxco.chi.il.us
Subject: My trip to Chicago is on!

Alicia, my travel request for your meeting was
approved.  Please send me the agenda.  Thanks.

& d
& q
Held 1 message in /usr/spool/mail/alicia
%
```

When you start **mail**, it prints a "message header" that shows whether each message is "new" (N) or "unread" (U), a message number, the sender, and when the message was sent. The current message is marked by ">". You can read any message by entering its number; if you use a command without out a number, the command acts on the current message. If you read a message and don't delete it, the message is automatically moved to a file called *mbox* in your home directory.

The output of **mail** says that the message was sent by Jerry on Thursday, November 4, at 2:25 pm. The ampersand (&) on the last line is the **mail** program prompt. Just as the UNIX shell prompt is a sign that the shell is waiting for you to enter a command, the mail prompt is a sign that the **mail** program is waiting for you to enter a mail command. Your mail prompt may consist of a single character. Learn the mail prompt on your system and enter one of the commands in Table 3-2. For instance, Alicia might have chosen to enter **r** to reply to Jerry before using **d** to delete his message.

Table 3-2: Mail Commands (at mail Prompt)

Command	Description
?	Display menu of mail commands.
#	Show message number #.
n	Display the next message.
p	Display current message.
d	Delete the message. Messages you don't delete are saved in *mbox*.
m *addrs*	Mail a message to the addresses *addrs*.
r	Reply to sender of current message.
R	Reply to sender and other recipients of current message.
s *file*	Save a message in the named *file*.
file *file*	Handle the messages in the named *file*.
file %	Handle the messages in your system mailbox.
h	Display summary of messages.
x	Exit the **mail** program, restoring any messages you have deleted.
q	Quit the **mail** program.

Exercise: Sending mail

You can practice sending mail to your friends in this exercise. List the users logged on to the system and choose a name. You can also use your user name to send mail to yourself. Enter the following message. Do not forget to press the RETURN key at the end of each line, and type CTRL-D on a line by itself when you're done.

List logged on users.   Enter **who**
Send mail to someone.   Enter **mail** *name*
                      Hi there!
                      I'm just trying
                      the mail program.
                      ^D

Customizing Your Account

As we saw earlier, your home directory includes a hidden file called *.profile* (*.login* and *.cshrc* if you are using the C shell). This file is the key to customizing your account, since it contains commands that are automatically executed whenever you log in.

Let's take a look at this file. Return to your home directory and display the file using **cat**. Your *.profile* might look something like this:

```
PATH=/bin:/usr/bin:/usr/local/bin:
export PATH
/usr/games/fortune
date
umask 002
stty erase ^H intr ^C
```

As you can see, the *.profile* contains commands to print a "fortune" and the date—just what happened earlier when we logged in! (*/usr/games/fortune* is a useless but entertaining program that prints a randomly selected saying from its collection. **fortune** isn't available on all systems.)

But what are these other commands?

* The line beginning PATH= gives the shell a list of directories in which to look for commands. This saves you the trouble of typing the complete pathname for each program you want to run. (Notice that */usr/games* isn't part of the path, and so we must use the absolute pathname to receive our daily dose of wisdom from the **fortune** command.)

* The **umask** command sets the default file permissions that will be assigned to all files that you create. Without going into the complexities of this command, let it suffice to say that a value of 022 will produce the permissions rw-r--r-- (read-write by owner, but read-only by everyone else), and 002 will produce rw-rw-r-- (read-write by owner and group, but read-only by everyone else). See one of the books in Appendix A or your UNIX documentation for details.

* The **stty** command sets your terminal control characters—for example, the erase and interrupt characters we discussed earlier.

You can execute any of these commands from the command line, as well. For example, to change your erase character from BACKSPACE (CTRL-H) to DEL (CTRL-?), you would enter:

```
% stty erase ^?
```

(The DEL key actually generates the control code CTRL-?, so that is what you will see on your screen, even if you press DEL.)

Now pressing DEL will backspace and erase characters you type. (If your account is already set up to use DEL as the erase character, reverse this example, and change the erase character to BACKSPACE.)

If you experiment with **stty**, you should be careful not to reset the erase or interrupt character to a character you'll need otherwise.

Just as you can execute the commands in *.profile* from the command line, the converse is true: any command that you can execute from the command line can be executed automatically when you log in by placing it in your *.profile*. (Running interactive commands like **mail** from your *.profile* isn't a good idea, though.)

It is premature at this point for you to edit your *.profile*, but it's good to know what it contains. Later, when you know more about the UNIX environment, feel free to add or change commands in this file.

4

File Management

Methods of Creating Files

You will usually create a text file with a text editor. An editor lets you add, change, and rearrange text easily. Two common editors in the UNIX environment are **vi** (pronounced "vee-eye") and **emacs** ("ee-macs").

Neither of those editors have the same features as popular word processing software on personal computers. Instead of being designed for making documents, envelopes, and so on, **vi** and **emacs** are sophisticated, extremely flexible editors for all kinds of text files: programs, e-mail messages, and so on. Many UNIX systems now also support easy-to-use word processors. Ask your System Administrator what's available.

Since several editor programs are available, you can choose the one you feel most comfortable with. **vi** is probably the best choice because it is available on almost all UNIX systems, but **emacs** is also widely available. The Nutshell Handbooks *Learning the vi Editor* and *Learning GNU Emacs* cover those editors in detail.

You can also create a file by using a UNIX feature called *input/output redirection*, as described in the next chapter. The output of a command can be sent directly to a file, thus creating a new file or a larger file from many smaller files.

File and Directory Names

As explained in Chapter 3, both files and directories are identified by their names. A directory is really just a special kind of file, so the rules for naming directories are the same as the rules for naming files.

Filenames may contain any character except /, which is reserved as the separator between files and directories in a pathname. Filenames are usually comprised of upper- and lowercase letters, numbers, "." (dot), and "_" (underscore). Other characters (including spaces) are legal in a filename—but they can be hard to use because the shell gives them special meanings. Unlike some operating systems, UNIX doesn't require a dot (.) in a filename; in fact, you can use as many as you want. For instance, the filenames *pizza* and *this.is.a.mess* are both legal.

Some UNIX systems limit filenames to 14 characters. Most newer systems allow much longer filenames.

A filename must be unique inside its directory, but other directories may have files with the same names. For example, you may have the files called *chap1* and *chap2* in the directory */users/carol/work* and also have files with the same names in */users/carol/play*.

File and Directory Wildcards

When you have a number of files named in series (for example, *chap1* to *chap12*) or filenames with common characters (like *aegis, aeon* and *aerie*), you can use *wildcards* (also called *metacharacters*) to specify many files at once. These special characters are * (asterisk), ? (question mark) and [ ] (square brackets). When used in a filename given as an argument to a command:

* An asterisk is replaced by any number of characters in a filename. For example, *ae** would match *aegis, aerie, aeon*, etc. if those files were in the same directory. You can use this to save typing for a single filename (for example, *al** for *alphabet.txt*) or to name many files at once (as in *ae**).

? A question mark is replaced by any single character (so *h?p* matches *hop* and *hip*, but not *help*).

[ ] Square brackets can surround a choice of characters you'd like to match. Any one of the characters between the brackets will be matched. For example, *[Cc]hapter* would match either *Chapter* or *chapter*, but *[ch]apter* would match either *capter* or *hapter*. Use a

hyphen to separate a range of consecutive characters. For example, *chap[1-3]* would match either *chap1*, *chap2*, or *chap3*.

The examples below demonstrate the use of wildcards.

```
% ls
chap10        chap2        chap5        cold
chap1a.old    chap3.old    chap6        haha
chap1b        chap4        chap7        oldjunk
% ls chap?
chap2     chap5     chap7
chap4     chap6
% ls chap[5-8]
chap5     chap6     chap7
% ls chap1?
chap10    chap1b
% ls *old
chap1a.old    chap3.old    cold
% ls *a*a*
chap1a.old    haha
```

Wildcards are useful for more than listing files. Most commands take more than one filename, and you can use wildcards to specify multiple files in the command line. For example, the command **more** is used to display a file on the screen. Let's say you want to display files *chap3.old* and *chap1a.old*. Instead of specifying these files individually, you could enter the command as:

```
% more *.old
```

This is equivalent to "**more chap1a.old chap3.old**".

Wildcards match directory names, too. For example, let's say you have sub-directories named *Jan*, *Feb*, *Mar*, and so on. Each has a file named *summary*. You could read all the summary files by typing "**more */summary**". That's equivalent to "**more Jan/summary Feb/summary ...**". (There's one important difference: the names will be alphabetized, so *Apr/summary* would be first in the list.)

Managing Your Files

The tree structure of the UNIX filesystem makes it easy to organize your files. After you make and edit some files, you may want to copy or move files from one directory to another, rename files to distinguish different versions of a file, or give several names to the same file. You may want to create new directories each time you start working on a different project.

A directory tree can get cluttered with old files you don't need. If you don't need a file or a directory, deleting it will free storage space on the disk.

Copying Files

If you're about to edit a file, you may want to save a copy of it first. Doing that makes it easy to get back the original version.

cp

The **cp** command can put a copy of a file into the same directory or into another directory. **cp** doesn't affect the original file, so it's a good way to keep an identical backup of a file.

To copy a file, use the command:

> **cp** *old new*

where *old* is a pathname to the original file and *new* is the pathname you want for the copy. For example, to copy the */etc/passwd* file into a file called *password* in your working directory, you would enter:

```
% cp /etc/passwd password
%
```

You can also use the form:

> **cp** *old old_dir*

This puts a copy of the original file *old* into an existing directory *old_dir*. The copy will have the same filename as the original.

If there's already a file with the same name as the copy, **cp** will replace the old file with your new copy. This is handy when you want to replace an old copy with a newer version, but it can cause trouble if you accidentally overwrite a copy you wanted to keep. To be safe, use **ls** to list the directory before you make a copy there. Also, many versions of **cp** have a *−i* (*i*nteractive) option that will ask before overwriting an existing file.

You can copy more than one file at a time to a single directory by listing the pathname of each file you want copied, with the destination directory at the end of the command line. You can use relative or absolute pathnames as well as simple filenames. For example, if your working directory was

/users/carol, to copy three files called *ch1*, *ch2* and *ch3* from */users/john* to a subdirectory called *work* (that's */users/carol/work*), you could enter:

```
% cp ../john/ch1 ../john/ch2 ../john/ch3 work
```

Or, you could use wildcards and let the shell find all the appropriate files. This time, let's add the −*i* option for safety:

```
% cp -i ../john/ch[1-3] work
cp: overwrite work/ch2? n
```

There was already a file named *ch2* in the *work* directory. When **cp** asked, I answered **n** to prevent copying *ch2*. Answering *y* would overwrite the old *ch2*.

You can also use the shorthand forms . and .. to refer to the working directory or its parent as the destination of the copy. For example:

```
% cp ../john/ch[1-3] .
```

will copy the specified files to the working directory.

Problem Checklist

✓ *The system says "cp: cannot copy file to itself".*

If the copy is in the same directory as the original, the filenames must be different.

✓ *The system says "cp: filename: no such file or directory".*

The system cannot find the file that you want to copy. Check for a typing mistake. Also remember to specify the pathname of any file not in the working directory.

✓ *The system says something like "cp: permission denied".*

You may not have permission to copy a file created by someone else or copy it into a directory that does not belong to you. Use **ls −l** to find the owner and the permissions for the file. If you feel that you should have permission to copy a file whose access is denied to you, ask the file's owner or the System Administrator to change the access modes for the file.

rcp

Some versions of UNIX have an **rcp** (remote copy) command for copying files between two computers. In general, you must have accounts on both computers. The syntax of **rcp** is like **cp**, but **rcp** also lets you add the remote hostname to the start of a file or directory pathname. The syntax of each argument is:

> *hostname:pathname*

hostname: is needed only for remote files. You can copy from a remote computer to the local computer, from the local to a remote, or between two remote computers.

For example, let's copy the files named *report.may* and *report.june* from your home directory on the computer named *giraffe*. Put the copies into your working directory (`.`) on the machine you're logged into now:

```
% rcp giraffe:report.may giraffe:report.june .
```

To use wildcards in the remote filenames, put quotation marks (`"name"`) around each remote name. For example, to copy all files from your *food/lunch* subdirectory on your *giraffe* account into your working directory on the local account, type:

```
% rcp "giraffe:food/lunch/*" .
```

Unlike **cp**, most versions of **rcp** do not have a *−i* safety option. Also, even if your system has **rcp**, your system administrator may not want you to use it for system security reasons. Another command, **ftp**, is more flexible and secure than **rcp**.

ftp

The command **ftp** (file transfer protocol) is a flexible way to copy files between two computers. Both computers don't need to be running UNIX, though they do need to be connected by a network that **ftp** can use. To start **ftp**, give the hostname of the remote computer:

> **ftp** *hostname*

ftp will prompt for your username and password on the remote computer. This is something like a remote login (see Chapter 1), but **ftp** doesn't start your usual shell. Instead, **ftp** prints its own prompt and uses a special set of commands for transferring files. The most important **ftp** commands are described in the following table.

Table 4-1: *Some ftp Commands*

Command	Description
put *filename*	Copies the file *filename* from your local computer to the remote computer.
get *filename*	Copies the file *filename* from the remote computer to your local computer.
cd *pathname*	Changes the working directory on the remote machine to *pathname* (ftp starts at your home directory on the remote machine).
lcd *pathname*	Changes ftp's working directory on the local machine to *pathname* (ftp starts at your working directory on the local computer). [Note that the ftp lcd command changes only ftp's working directory. After you quit ftp, your shell's working directory will not have changed.]
dir	Lists the remote directory (like ls -l).
binary	Tells ftp to copy the following file(s) without translation. This preserves pictures, sound or other data.
ascii	Transfers plain text files, translating data if needed.
quit	Ends the ftp session and takes you back to a shell prompt.

Here's an example. Carol uses **ftp** to copy the file *todo* from the *work* sub-directory on her account on the remote computer *rhino*:

```
% ftp rhino
Connected to rhino.zoo.com.
Name (rhino:carol): csmith
Password:
ftp> cd work
ftp> dir
total 3
-rw-r--r--  1 csmith    mgmt     47 Feb  5  1993 for.ed
-rw-r--r--  1 csmith    mgmt    264 Oct 11 12:18 message
-rw-r--r--  1 csmith    mgmt    724 Nov 20 14:53 todo
ftp> get todo
ftp> quit
% ls
afile    ch2    somefile    todo
```

We've covered the most basic **ftp** commands here. For more information, see the Nutshell Handbook *The Whole Internet User's Guide and Catalog*.

Renaming and Moving Files

You will sometimes need to change the name of a file; for example, when you have made a lot of changes to it or when you want to set a copy apart from the original file. To rename a file, use the **mv** (move) command. The **mv** command can also move a file from one directory to another.

mv

The **mv** command has the same syntax as the **cp** command:

> **mv** *old new*

old is the old name of the file and *new* is the new name. **mv** will write over existing files, which is handy for updating old versions of a file; if you don't want that to happen, though, be sure that the new name is unique. If your **cp** has a *–i* option for safety, your **mv** probably has one too.

```
% mv chap1 intro
%
```

The above example changed the name of the file *chap1* to *intro*. If you list your files with **ls**, you will see that the old name *chap1* has disappeared.

The **mv** command can also move a file from one directory to another. As with the **cp** command, if you want to keep the same filename, you only need to give **mv** the name of the destination directory.

Finding Files

If your account has lots of files, organizing those files into subdirectories can help you find the files later. Sometimes you may not remember which subdirectory has a file. The **find** command can search for files in many ways; we'll look at two of them.

Change to your home directory so **find** will start its search there. Then carefully enter one of the two **find** commands below. (The syntax is strange and ugly—but **find** does the job!)

```
% cd
% find . -name 'chap*' -print
./chap2
./old/chap10b
% find . -mtime -2 -print
./work/to_do
```

The first command looked in your working (home) directory and all its subdirctories for files whose names start with *chap*. The second command looked in the same places for all files that have been created or modified in the last two days (**-mtime -2**). The relative pathnames start with a dot (**. /**), the name of the working directory, which you can ignore. To learn much more about **find**, read your online documentation or read the chapter about it in *UNIX Power Tools*.

Creating Directories

It is usually convenient to put all files related to one topic in the same directory. If you were writing a spy novel, you probably wouldn't want your files containing your ideas mixed up with phone listings for restaurants. You would create two directories; one for all the chapters in your novel (*spy*, for example), and another for restaurants (*boston.dine*). Grouping related files into their own directories will organize your filesystem.

mkdir

To create a new directory, use the mkdir command. The format is:

> **mkdir** *dirname(s)*

dirname is the name of the new directory. To continue our example, you would enter:

```
% mkdir spy boston.dine
```

Removing Files and Directories

There will come a time when you no longer need a particular file or directory. You may have already finished working on it and see no need to keep it on your filesystem, or the contents may be obsolete. Periodically removing unwanted files and directories will free storage space on your disk.

rm

The **rm** command removes unwanted files so you can clean up your directory tree. The syntax is simple:

> **rm** *filename(s)*

rm removes the named files, as shown in the following examples:

```
% ls
chap10       chap2        chap5    cold
chap1a.old   chap3.old    chap6    haha
chap1b       chap4        chap7    oldjunk
% rm *.old chap10
% ls
chap1b     chap4     chap6    cold    oldjunk
chap2      chap5     chap7    haha
% rm c*
% ls
haha      oldjunk
%
```

Make sure you are deleting the correct files when you use wildcards in the **rm** command. If you accidentally remove a file you need, you cannot recover it unless you have a backup copy in another directory or on tape.

CAUTION

Do not type "rm *" carelessly. If you do, you will delete all the files in your working directory.

Here's another easy mistake to make: You want to type a command like "rm c*" (remove all filenames starting with "c") but instead type "rm c *" (remove the file named "c" and all files!).

It is good practice to list the files with **ls** before you remove them. Or, if you use **rm**'s *−i* (*i*nteractive) option, **rm** will ask you whether you want to remove each file.

rmdir

Just as you can create new directories, you can also remove them with the **rmdir** command. As a precaution, the **rmdir** command will not let you delete directories that contain any files or subdirectories: the directory must first be empty.

The syntax of the command is:

> **rmdir** *dirname*

If a directory you try to remove does contain files, you will get a message like "rmdir: *dirname* not empty."

To delete a directory that contains some files:

1. Enter **cd** *dirname* to get into the directory you want to delete.
2. Enter **rm *** to remove all files in that directory.
3. Enter **cd ..** to go to the parent directory.
4. Enter **rmdir** *dirname* to remove the unwanted directory.

Problem Checklist

✓ *I still get the message "dirname not empty" even after I've deleted all the files.*

Use **ls –a** to check that there are no hidden files (names beginning with a period) other than . and .. (the working directory and its parent). The command **rm .[a–zA–Z] .??*** is good for cleaning up hidden files.

Using **mkdir** and **rmdir**, you can build and remodel your own file hierarchy.

Printing Files

There are two parts to printing: formatting and actual printing. If you are using a word processor, formatting is generally considered a phase of editing. If you are using a text editor, formatting is a phase of printing.

Many versions of UNIX include two powerful text formatters, **nroff** and **troff**. They are much too complex to describe here. However, before we take up printing proper, let's look at a simple formatting program called **pr**.

pr

The **pr** command provides minor formatting of files on the terminal screen or for a printer. For example, if you have a long list of names in a file, you can format it on-screen so that two or more columns of names are produced for readability.

The syntax is:

> **pr** *option(s) filename(s)*

pr changes the format of the file only on the screen or on the printed copy; it doesn't modify the original file. Table 4-2 lists some **pr** options.

Table 4-2: Useful Options of pr

Option	Description
–*k*	Produces *k* columns of output.
–d	Double-spaces the output (not on all **pr** versions).
–h *"header"*	Takes the next item as a report *header*.
–t	Eliminates printing of header or top/bottom margins.

Other options allow you to specify the width of the columns, set the page length, and so on. To see how **pr** works, let's process the file named *food*. Its contents are shown just as they appear in the file.

```
Sweet Tooth
Bangkok Wok
Mandalay
Afghani Cuisine
Isle of Java
Big Apple Deli
Sushi and Sashimi
Tio Pepe's Peppers
```

Using **pr** options, we will specify a two-column report with the header "Restaurants."

```
% pr -2 -h "Restaurants" food

Nov  7  9:58 1993   Restaurants    Page 1

Sweet Tooth                        Isle of Java
Bangkok Wok                        Big Apple Deli
Mandalay                           Sushi and Sashimi
Afghani Cuisine                    Tio Pepe's Peppers
                          .
                          .
                          .

%
```

The output is separated into 2-column pages with the date and time, header (or name of the file, if header is not supplied), and page number. To send this output to the printer instead of the terminal screen, you have to create a pipe to the printer program, **lp** or **lpr**. The following section describes **lp** and **lpr**; Chapter 5 covers pipes.

lp and lpr

If you have a long file, it may be best to print it so you can see it all on paper. The command **lp** or **lpr** is used to print a hardcopy of a file. The format is as follows:

> **lp** *file1 file2* ...
> **lpr** *file1 file2* ...

The printer on your UNIX system is usually shared by a group of users. After you enter the command to print a file, the shell prompt returns to the screen and you can enter another command. However, seeing the prompt doesn't mean that your file has been printed. Your file has been added to the printer queue to be printed in turn.

Your system administrator has probably set up a default printer at your site. To print a file on the default printer, use the **lp** or **lpr** command as in the example below.

```
% lp bills
request id is laserp-525  (1 file)
%
```

lp displays a unique ID that can be used to cancel the printing request or to check its status; if you need ID numbers for **lpr** jobs, use the **lpq** command (see below). The file *bills* will be sent to a printer called *laserp*. The ID number of the request is "laserp-525".

lp and **lpr** have several options. Table 4-3 lists three of them.

Table 4-3: Useful Options of lp and lpr

Option		Description
lp	lpr	
–d*printer*	–P*printer*	Use given *printer* name if there is more than one printer at your site. The printer names are assigned by the system administrator.
–n#	–#	Print # copies of the file.
–m	–m	Notify sender by e-mail when the printing is done.

If **lp** or **lpr** does not work at your site, ask other users for the appropriate printer command, and for the printer locations, so you know where to pick up your output.

Problem Checklist

✓ *My printout has not come out.*

1. Check to see if the printer is currently printing. If it is, other users may have made a request to the same printer ahead of you and your file should be printed in turn. The section below explains how to check the print requests.

2. If no file is printing, check the printer's physical connections and power switch. The printer may also be hung. If it is, ask your system administrator what to do.

Viewing the Printer Queue

If you want to find out how many files are ahead of yours in the printer queue, you can use the command **lpstat** (for **lp**) or **lpq** (for **lpr**). The **cancel** command lets you terminate a printing request made by **lp**; **lprm** cancels jobs from **lpr**.

lpstat and lpq

The **lpstat** command displays the contents of the printer queue: the request IDs, the owners, the sizes of the files, the times when the jobs were sent for printing, and the status of the requests, in that order. Use **lpstat –o** if you want to see all output requests rather than just your own. Requests are shown in the order that they will be printed.

```
% lpstat -o
laserp-573  john   128865  Nov 7  11:27  on laserp
laserp-574  grace  82744   Nov 7  11:28
laserp-575  john   23347   Nov 7  11:35
%
```

The first entry shows that the request "laserp-573" is currently printing on *laserp*. The exact format and amount of information given about the printer queue may differ from system to system. If the printer queue is empty, **lpstat** will say "No entries" or simply give you back the shell prompt.

lpq gives slightly different information than **lpstat –o**:

```
% lpq
laserp is ready and printing
Rank    Owner   Job  Files                 Total Size
active  john    573  report.ps             128865 bytes
1st     grace   574  ch03.ps ch04.ps       82744 bytes
2nd     john    575  standard input        23347 bytes
%
```

The first line tells the printer status. If the printer is disabled or out of paper, you may see different messages on this first line. The "active" job, the one being printed, is listed first. The "Job" number is like the **lpstat** request ID.

cancel and lprm

cancel will terminate a printing request from the **lp** command. **lprm** terminates **lpr** requests. You can specify either the ID of the request (displayed by **lp** or **lpq**) or the name of the printer.

If you don't have the request ID, get it from **lpstat** or **lpq**. Then use **cancel** or **lprm**. Specifying the request ID cancels the request, even if it is currently printing. To cancel whatever request is currently printing, regardless of its ID, simply enter **cancel** and the printer name:

```
% cancel laserp-575
request "laserp-575" cancelled
% cancel laserp
request "laserp-573" cancelled
```

The **lprm** command will cancel the active job if it belongs to you. Otherwise, you can give job numbers as arguments, or a dash (–) to remove all of your jobs:

```
% lprm 575
dfA575diamond dequeued
cfA575diamond dequeued
```

lpr tells you the actual filenames removed from the printer queue (which are probably of no use to you).

Exercise: Manipulating files

In this exercise, you'll create, rename and delete files. Find out if your site has one or more printers and the appropriate command to use for printing.

Go to home directory.	Enter **cd**
Copy distant file to working directory.	Enter **cp /etc/passwd myfile**
Create new directory.	Enter **mkdir temp**
Move file to new directory.	Enter **mv myfile temp**
Change working directory.	Enter **cd temp**
Copy file to working directory.	Enter **cp myfile myfile.two**
Print the file.	Enter **lp myfile**

List filenames with wildcard.	Enter **ls -l myfile***
Remove files.	Enter **rm myfile***
Go up to parent directory.	Enter **cd ..**
Remove directory.	Enter **rmdir temp**
Verify that directory was removed.	Enter **ls -l**

5

Redirecting I/O

Standard Input and Standard Output

Many UNIX commands read input (such as a file) and write output.

In general, if no filename is specified in a command, the shell takes whatever you type on your keyboard as input to the command (after you press the first RETURN to start the command running, that is). Your terminal keyboard is the command's *standard input*.

When a command has finished running, the results are usually displayed on your terminal screen. The terminal screen is the command's *standard output*. By default, each command takes its input from the standard input and sends the results to the standard output.

These two default cases of input/output can be varied. This is called *input/output redirection*. You can use a given file as input to a command that doesn't normally accept filenames by using the "<" operator. For example, the following command mails the contents of the file *to_do* to *bigboss@corp*:

```
% mail bigboss@corp < to_do
%
```

You can also write the results of a command to a named file or some other device instead of displaying it on the screen using the ">" operator.

Input/output redirection is one of the nicest features of UNIX because of its tremendous power and flexibility.

Putting Text in a File

Instead of always letting the output of a command come to the screen, you can redirect output into a file. This is useful when you have a lot of output that would be difficult to read on the screen or when you put files together to create a bigger file. As we've seen, the **cat** command can be used for displaying a short file. It can also be used to put text into a file, or to create a bigger file out of smaller files.

The > operator

When you append the notation "> *filename*" to the end of a command, the results of the command are diverted from the standard output to the named file. The > symbol is known as the *output redirection operator.*

When you use **cat** with this operator, the contents of the file that are normally displayed on the standard output are diverted into a new file. This becomes clear in the example below.

```
% cat /etc/passwd > password
% cat password
root::0:0:Root:/:/bin/sh
daemon:NONE:1:1:Admin:/:
           .
           .
           .
john::128:50:John Doe:/usr/john:/bin/sh
%
```

An example in Chapter 3 showed how "**cat /etc/passwd**" simply displays the file */etc/passwd* on the screen. The example above adds the > operator. Instead of displaying the results of the command on the terminal screen, the contents are diverted to a file called *password* in the working directory. Displaying the file *password* shows that its contents are the same as the file */etc/passwd*. The effect is the same as the copy command "**cp /etc/passwd password**".

The > redirection operator can be used with any command that sends text to its standard output—not just with **cat**. For example:

```
% who > users
% date > today
% ls
password   today   users   ...
```

You have sent the output of **who** to a file called *users* and the output of **date** to a file called *today*. Listing your directory shows that the two new files have been created. Look at these files to see the output produced by the commands **who** and **date**.

```
% cat users
tim      tty1     Aug 12   07:30
john     tty4     Aug 12   08:26
% cat today
Thu Aug 12 08:36:09 EST 1993
%
```

You can also create a small text file using the **cat** command and the > operator. We told you earlier to press CTRL-D if you accidentally enter **cat** without a filename. This is because the **cat** command alone takes whatever you type on the keyboard as input. Thus, the command

>   **cat** > *filename*

takes input from the keyboard and redirects it to a file. Try the example below:

```
% cat > to_do
Finish report by noon
Lunch with Xannie
Swim at 5:30
^D
%
```

cat takes the text that you typed as input, and the > operator redirects it to a file called *to_do*. Type CTRL-D on a new line by itself to signal the end of the text. You should get a shell prompt.

You can also create a bigger file out of many smaller files using the **cat** command and the > operator. The form:

>   **cat** *file1 file2* > *newfile*

creates a file *newfile*, consisting of *file1* followed by *file2*.

```
% cat today to_do > diary
% cat diary
Thu Aug 12 08:36:09 EST 1993
Finish report by noon
Lunch with Xannie
Swim at 5:30
%
```

CAUTION

If you are using the > (output redirection) operator, you should be careful not to overwrite the contents of a file accidentally. Your system may let you redirect output to an existing file. If so, the old file will be deleted (or, in UNIX lingo, "clobbered"). It is your own responsibility to be careful not to overwrite a much-needed file.

If you are using the C or Korn shell, there is a mechanism to protect you from the risk of overwriting an important file. In the C shell, use the command **set noclobber**, typed at a prompt or in your *.cshrc* file. The Korn shell command is **set –o noclobber**; enter it at a prompt or put it in your *.profile* file. After that, the shell will not allow you to redirect onto an existing file and overwrite its contents.

This does not protect against overwriting by UNIX commands like **cp**; it works only with the > redirection operator. For more protection, you can set UNIX file access permissions.

The >> operator

You can also append information to the end of an existing file, instead of replacing its contents, by using the >> (append redirection) operator in place of the > (output redirection) operator.

> **cat** *file2* >> *file1*

appends the contents of *file2* to the end of *file1*.

```
% cat users >> diary
% cat diary
Thu Aug 12 08:36:09 EST 1993
Finish report by noon
Lunch with Xannie
Swim at 5:30
tim      tty1     Aug 12   07:30
john     tty4     Aug 12   08:26
%
```

Pipes and Filters

In addition to redirecting input/output to a named file, you can connect two commands together so that the output from one program becomes the input of the next command. Two or more commands connected in this way form a *pipe*. To make a pipe, type a vertical bar (|) on the command line between two commands. When a pipe is set up between two commands, the standard output of the command to the left of the pipe symbol becomes the standard input of the command to the right of the pipe symbol. Any two programs can form a pipe as long as the first program writes to standard output and the second program reads from standard input.

When a program takes its input from another program, performs some operation on that input, and writes the result to the standard output (or possibly pipes the result to yet another program), it is referred to as a *filter*. One of the most common uses of filters is to modify output. Just as a common filter culls unwanted items, the UNIX filters can be used to restructure output.

Almost all UNIX commands can be used to form pipes. Some programs that are commonly used as filters are described below. Note that these programs are not used only as filters or parts of pipes. They are also useful as individual commands.

grep

grep is a useful program that searches a file or files for lines that contain strings of a certain pattern. The syntax is:

> **grep** *"pattern" files*

The name "grep" derives from the **ed** (a UNIX line editor) command **g/re/p** which means "*g*lobally search for a *re*gular expression and *p*rint all lines containing it." A *regular expression* combines a string of text with some special characters used for pattern matching. When you learn more about text editing, you can use regular expressions to specify complex patterns of text.

The simplest use of **grep** is to look for a pattern consisting of a fixed character string. For example, it can be used in a pipe so that only those lines of the input files containing a given string are sent to the standard output. If you don't give **grep** a filename to read, it reads its standard input; that's the way all filter programs work:

```
% ls -l | grep "Aug"
-rw-rw-rw-   1 john   doc      11008 Aug  6 14:10 ch02
-rw-rw-rw-   1 john   doc       8515 Aug  6 15:30 ch07
-rw-rw-r--   1 john   doc       2488 Aug 15 10:51 intro
-rw-rw-r--   1 carol  doc       1605 Aug 23 07:35 macros
%
```

The simple pipe in our example looks for all lines in the **ls -l** output that contain the string "Aug" (that is, they were last modified in August) and sends those lines to the terminal screen.

grep has a number of options that allow you to modify the search. Some of these are given in Table 5-1.

Table 5-1: Useful grep Options

Option	Description
–v	Print all lines that do not match pattern.
–n	Print the matched line and its line number.
–l	Print only the names of files with matching lines (letter "l").
–c	Print only the count of matching lines.
–i	Match either upper or lowercase.

Next, let's use a regular expression that tells **grep** to find lines with "carol" followed later in the line by "Aug". (For more about regular expressions, see the references in Appendix A.)

```
% ls -l | grep "carol.*Aug"
-rw-rw-r--   1 carol doc      1605 Aug 23 07:35 macros
%
```

sort

The **sort** program arranges the contents of a file alphabetically or numerically. The example below sorts the first field or column of the file, *food*, alphabetically.

```
% sort food
Afghani Cuisine
Bangkok Wok
Big Apple Deli
Isle of Java
Mandalay
Sushi and Sashimi
Sweet Tooth
```

sort arranges lines of text alphabetically by default. There are many options that control the sort order. Some of these are given in Table 5-2.

Table 5-2: Useful sort Options

Option	Description
–n	Sort numerically (example: 10 will sort after 2), ignore blanks and tabs.
–r	Reverse the order of sort.
–f	Sort upper- and lowercase together.
+x	Ignore first x fields when sorting.

More than two commands may be linked up into a pipe. Taking a previous pipe example using **grep**, we can further sort the files modified in August by order of size. The following pipe consists of the commands **ls**, **grep**, and **sort**:

```
% ls -l | grep "Aug" | sort +4n
-rw-rw-r--  1 carol  doc      1605 Aug 23 07:35 macros
-rw-rw-r--  1 john   doc      2488 Aug 15 10:51 intro
-rw-rw-rw-  1 john   doc      8515 Aug  6 15:30 ch07
-rw-rw-rw-  1 john   doc     11008 Aug  6 14:10 ch02
%
```

This pipe sorts all files in your directory modified in August by order of size, and prints them to the terminal screen. The **sort** option *+4n* tells UNIX to skip four fields (fields are separated by blanks) then sort the lines in numeric order. Both **grep** and **sort** are used here as filters to modify the output of the **ls -l** command.

pg and more

The **more** and **pg** programs that you saw earlier can also be used as filters. A long output would normally zip by you on the screen, but if you run a file through **more** or **pg** as a filter, the display stops after each screenful of text.

Let's assume that you have a long directory listing. To make it easier to read the sorted file, pipe the output through **more**:

```
% ls -l | grep "Aug" | sort +4n | more
-rw-rw-r--  1 carol  doc      1605 Aug 23 07:35 macros
-rw-rw-r--  1 john   doc      2488 Aug 15 10:51 intro
-rw-rw-rw-  1 john   doc      8515 Aug  6 15:30 ch07
-rw-rw-r--  1 john   doc     14827 Aug  9 12:40 ch03
              .
              .
              .
-rw-rw-rw-  1 john   doc     16867 Aug  6 15:56 ch05
--More--(74%)
```

The screen will fill up with one screenful of text consisting of lines sorted by order of file size. At the bottom of the screen is the **more** prompt where you can type a command to move through the sorted text. To continue reading the file, you can press any of the keys listed in the discussion of the **more** program.

Exercise: Redirecting input/output

In the following exercises you'll redirect output, create a simple pipe, and use filters to modify output.

Redirect output to a file.	Enter **who > users**
Sort output of a command.	Enter **who	sort**
Append sorted output to a file.	Enter **who	sort >> users**
Display output to screen.	Enter **more users** or **pg users**
Display long output to screen.	Enter **ls -l /bin	more** or **ls -l /bin	pg**
Format and print a file with **pr**	Enter **pr users	lp** or **pr users	lpr**

6

Multi-tasking

Suppose you are running a command that will take a long time to process. On a single-tasking system like MS-DOS, you would enter the command and wait for the system prompt to return, telling you that you could enter a new command. In UNIX, however, there is a way to enter new commands in the "foreground" while one or more commands are still running in the "background." This is called *background processing*.

When you enter a command as a background process, the shell prompt reappears immediately so that you can enter a new command. The original command will still be running in the "background," but you can use the system to do other things during that time. Depending on your system and your shell, you may even be able to log off and let the background process run to completion.

Running a Command in the Background

Running a command as a background process is most often done to free up a terminal when you know that the command will take a long time to run.

To run a command as a background process, add the "&" character at the end of the command line before you press the RETURN key. The shell will then assign and display a process ID number for the command. This is shown in the example below:

```
% nroff -ms chap1 > chap1.out &
[1] 29890
%
```

(**nroff** is a program used to format documents for printing. It is used here as an example because text formatting usually takes a while, and so is an ideal candidate for background processing. See your UNIX documentation for details on **nroff**.)

The process ID (PID) for the command is 29890. The process ID is useful when you want to check the status of a background process or, if you need to, cancel it. You don't need to remember the process ID, because there are UNIX commands (explained below) to check on the processes you have running. In some shells, a status line will be printed on your screen when the background process finishes.

In the C shell, you can put an entire sequence of commands separated by semicolons into the background by putting an & at the end of the entire command line. In the Bourne and Korn shells, enclose the command sequence in parentheses before typing the ampersand:

> (*command1 ; command2*)&

On many systems, the C and Korn shells support an additional feature called *job control*. You can use the *suspend character* (usually CTRL-Z) to suspend a program running in the foreground. The program will pause and you'll get a new shell prompt. You can then do anything else you like, including putting the suspended program into the background using the **bg** command. The **fg** command will bring a background process to the foreground.

For example, you might start **sort** running on a big file, and, after a minute, want to send e-mail. You stop **sort**, then put it in the background. The shell prints a message, then another shell prompt. You send mail while **sort** runs.

```
% sort hugefile1 hugefile2 > sorted
      ...time goes by...
CTRL-Z
Stopped
% bg
[1]    sort hugefile1 hugefile2 > sorted &
% mail eduardo@nacional.cl
      ...
```

Checking on a Process

If you find that a background process is taking too long to execute, or you change your mind and want to stop a process, you can check the status of the process and even cancel it if it is no longer wanted.

ps

When you enter the single-word command **ps**, you can see how long a process has been running. The output of **ps** also tells you the process ID of the background process and the terminal from which it was run.

```
% ps
PID     TTY     TIME    COMMAND
8048    020     0:12    sh
8699    020     0:02    ps
%
```

In its basic form, **ps** lists the following:

Process ID (PID)	A unique number assigned by UNIX to the process.
Terminal line (TTY)	The terminal number from which the process was started.
Run time (TIME)	The amount of computer time (in minutes and seconds) that the process has used.
Command (COMMAND)	The name of the process.

At the very least, **ps** will list one process: **ps** itself. You should also see the names of any other programs you have run in the background and the name of your shell (**sh**, **csh**, etc.).

You should be aware that there are two types of programs on UNIX systems: compiled programs and shell scripts. Compiled programs are written in a programming language like C or Pascal. Shell scripts are sequences of stored commands. If you execute a shell script, you will see an additional **sh** (or **csh**) command in the **ps** listing, as well as all of the commands that are executed by the shell script.

Shells with job control have a command called **jobs**, which lists all background processes. As mentioned above, there are commands to change the foreground/background status of jobs. There are other job control commands as well. See one of the references in Appendix A for details.

Cancelling a Process

You realize, after some time, that you have made a mistake in putting a process in the background. Or after checking on the status of the process, you decide that it is taking too long to execute. You can cancel a background process if you know its process ID.

kill

The **kill** command is used to stop a process from further execution. The format of the command is:

> **kill** *PID(s)*

kill terminates the designated process IDs (shown under the PID heading in the **ps** listing). If you do not know the process ID, do a **ps** first to display the status of your processes.

In the following example, the "**sleep** *n*" command simply causes a process to "go to sleep" for *n* number of seconds. We enter two commands, **sleep** and **who**, on the same line, as a background process.

```
% (sleep 60; who)&
[1] 21087
% ps
  PID    TTY    TIME   COMMAND
 20055   4     0:10   sh
 21087   4     0:01   sh
 21088   4     0:00   sleep
 21089   4     0:02   ps
% kill 21088
Terminated
% tom      tty2    Aug 30   11:27
grace     tty4    Aug 30   12:24
tim       tty5    Aug 30   07:52
dale      tty7    Aug 30   14:34
```

We decided that 60 seconds was too long a time to wait for the output of **who**. The **ps** listing shows that **sleep** has the process ID number 21088, so we use this PID to kill the **sleep** process. You will see the message: "Terminated."

The **who** command is executed immediately, since it is no longer waiting on **sleep**; it lists the users logged into the system.

Problem Checklist

✓ *The process didn't die when I told it to.*

Some processes can be hard to kill. If a normal kill of these processes is not working, enter "**kill -9** *PID*". This is a sure kill and can destroy almost anything, including the shell that is interpreting it.

In addition, if you've run a shell script, you may not be able to kill all dependent processes by killing the **sh** that got it all started; you may need to kill them individually. However, killing a process that is feeding data into a pipe will generally kill any processes receiving that data.

7

Where to Go From Here

Standard UNIX Documentation

Now that you've come to the end of this learning guide, you should be able to go through a typical UNIX session with ease. At this point, you might want to know the various options to the commands we've introduced and the many other UNIX commands. You're ready to consult your system's documentation.

Different system manufacturers have adapted UNIX documentation in different ways. However, almost all UNIX documentation is derived from a manual originally called the *UNIX Programmer's Manual*. One section you'll want to consult lists general UNIX commands like **who** and **ls**. There's probably another section with tutorials and extended documentation.

Online Documentation

Many UNIX installations (especially larger systems with plenty of disk space) have individual manual pages stored on the computer; users can read them online.

If you want to know the correct syntax for entering a command or the particular features of a program, enter the command **man** and the name of the command. The format is:

> **man** *command*

For example, if you want to find information about the program **mail**, which allows you to send messages to other users, you would enter:

```
% man mail
       .
       .
       .
%
```

The output of **man** may be filtered through the **more** command automatically. If it isn't, just pipe the output of **man** to **more** (or **pg**).

After you enter the command, the screen will fill up with text. Press SPACE to go on to the next screen.

Some systems also have a command called **apropos** or **man -k** to help you locate a command if you have an idea of what it does but are not sure of its correct name. Enter **apropos** followed by a descriptive word; you'll get a list of commands that might help.

Interesting Things to Learn

Out of the hundreds of UNIX commands that have been developed, the commands for editing files are probably among the first that you should learn. As you become more familiar with other UNIX commands, you can customize your working environment and also create commands to do just what you need.

Editors

Word processing is one of the most frequently used functions of a computer. Whether you are writing a computer program or a chapter of a novel, basic editing is sure to be the first step.

It will help you become more productive if you devote some time to learning the UNIX editor on your system. This is usually **vi** or **emacs**. Whether you use **vi**, **emacs**, or another editor, you will have to learn the special commands associated with the editor that will allow you to search, add and delete characters or lines. You will find that some commands come more easily to you than others. Don't try to learn all the commands. Use the commands most comfortable for and useful to you.

Shell Programming

We have mentioned earlier that the shell is the system's command interpreter. It reads each command you enter at your terminal and performs the operation that you called for. The System Administrator decides the type of shell that runs when you log in to your account.

The shell is just an ordinary program that can be called by a UNIX command. However, it contains some features (like variables, control structures, and so on) that make it similar to a programming language. You can save a series of shell commands in a file, called a *shell script*, to accomplish specialized functions.

Programming the shell should be attempted only when you are reasonably confident of your ability to use UNIX commands. UNIX is quite a powerful tool and its capabilities become more apparent when you try your hand at shell programming.

Take time to learn the basics. Then, when you're faced with a new task, take time to browse through references to find programs or options that will help you get the job done more easily. Once you've done that, learn how to build shell scripts so that you never have to type a complicated command sequence more than once.

Reading List

This section lists a few good books in several areas.

General UNIX Books

- *A Student's Guide to UNIX* by Harley Hahn; McGraw-Hill; ISBN 0-07-025511-3; 1993. Not just for students, this is a complete and very readable guide to UNIX and networking.

- *UNIX Power Tools* by Jerry Peek, Tim O'Reilly, Mike Loukides, and others; O'Reilly & Associates and Random House Electronic Publishing; ISBN 0-679-79073-X; 1993. A huge collection of tips, techniques, and concepts for making intermediate users into advanced users. Comes with a CD-ROM full of useful software.

- *UNIX in a Nutshell (System V & Solaris 2.0)* by Daniel Gilly and the staff of O'Reilly & Associates; ISBN 1-56592-001-5; 1992. From user commands to programmers' utilities, this book covers UNIX with concise descriptions and illustrative examples. Aimed at System V but also includes Berkeley features.

- *SCO UNIX in a Nutshell* by Ellie Cutler and the staff of O'Reilly & Associates; ISBN 1-56592-037-6; 1994. Like *UNIX in a Nutshell* (above), a complete reference for the SCO version of UNIX.

- *The UNIX Programming Environment* by Brian Kernighan and Rob Pike; Prentice-Hall; ISBN 0-13-937681-X; 1984. This is a fast-paced introduction to UNIX and its philosophy. It's old, and it's oriented toward programmers, but it's a favorite of hard-core UNIX users: a real classic.

Text Processing

- *Learning the vi Editor* by Linda Lamb; O'Reilly & Associates; ISBN 0-937175-67-6; 1992. A complete introduction to **vi**.

- *Learning GNU Emacs* by Deb Cameron & Bill Rosenblatt; O'Reilly & Associates; ISBN 0-937175-84-6; 1992. Emacs doesn't come with many versions of UNIX, but a lot of users find and install it—especially the version called GNU Emacs.

- *sed & awk* by Dale Dougherty; O'Reilly & Associates; ISBN 0-937175-59-5; 1992. From the very basics for beginners to the arcane details for serious users, this book explains two of the most versatile UNIX utilities for editing and processing text and data.

Electronic Mail and Communications

- *The Whole Internet User's Guide & Catalog* by Ed Krol; O'Reilly & Associates; ISBN 1-56592-063-5; 1994. The definitive guide to this worldwide network for e-mail, news, and many other services.

- *UNIX Communications* by Brian Costales and others; Howard Sams; ISBN 0-672-22511-5; 1990. A user's guide to all kinds of UNIX communications.

- *The Internet Companion* by Tracy La Quey and Jeanne C. Ryer; Addison-Wesley; ISBN 0-201-62224-6; 1992. Introduction to the Internet, its language, culture, and etiquette.

- *Connecting to the Internet: An O'Reilly Buyer's Guide* by Susan Estrada; O'Reilly & Associates; ISBN 1-56592-061-9; 1993. How to connect your computer, big or small, to the Internet.

- *!%@:: A Directory of Electronic Mail Addressing & Networks* by Donnalyn Frey & Rick Adams; O'Reilly & Associates; ISBN 1-56592-031-7; 1993. A directory of over 180 major networks connected to the Internet: their capabilities, contact information, and complete indexing.

Shells and Shell Programming

- *UNIX Shell Programming* by Stephen G. Kochan and Patrick H. Wood; Howard Sams; ISBN 0-672-48448-X; 1990. An excellent introduction to Bourne and Korn Shell programming with lots of illustrative examples.

- *Learning the Korn Shell* by Bill Rosenblatt; O'Reilly & Associates; ISBN 1-56592-054-6; 1993. A guide to using and programming this popular shell.

- *The UNIX C Shell Field Guide* by Gail and Paul Anderson; Prentice-Hall; ISBN 0-13-937468-X; 1986. A good guide to the nooks and crannies.

The X Window System

- *X Window System User's Guide, Volume 3, OSF/Motif edition*; Valerie Quercia and Tim O'Reilly; O'Reilly & Associates; ISBN 1-56592-015-5; 1993. A thorough guide to using and customizing the OSF/Motif graphical interface to X. Easy for beginners, but thorough enough to be a guide for experienced users.

Reference

Commands and Their Meanings

cancel *request*	Cancel an **lp** print request.
cat *files*	Display one or more files.
cd	Change to home directory.
cd *pathname*	Change working directory to *pathname*.
cp *old new*	Copy *old* file to *new* file.
date	Display current date and time.
grep *"pattern" files*	Show lines matching *pattern* in *files*.
kill *PID*	End process *PID*.
lp *files*	Send *files* to default printer.
lpq	Check requests on **lpr** printer queue.
lpr *files*	Send *files* to default printer.
lprm *request*	Cancel an **lpr** print request.
lpstat	Check requests on **lpstat** printer queue.
ls	List names of files in working directory.
mail	Read your own mail.
mail *user*	Send mail to *user*.
man *command*	Display manual page of *command*.
mkdir *pathname*	Create a new directory with *pathname*.
more *files*	Display one screenful of each *file* at a time.
mv *old new*	Move or rename *old* file to *new* file.
pg *files*	Display one screenful of each *file* at a time.
ps	List your processes and their PIDs.
pwd	Print working (current) directory name.
rm *files*	Remove *files*.
rmdir *pathname*	Remove empty directory with *pathname*.
sort *files*	Sort lines of *files*.
who	List users currently on system.
who am i	Display listing for this session.

Special Symbols

Symbol	Description
|	Set up a pipe.
>	Redirect output to a file.
<	Redirect input from a file.
>>	Append output to an existing file.
/	Separator used in pathnames.
&	Process command in the background.
*	Match any number of characters in filename.
?	Match any single character in filename.
[]	Match any one of the enclosed characters in filename.

Index

About the Author

Grace Todino is currently residing in Oman. While working as a technical writer at O'Reilly & Associates, Inc., Grace was one of the original authors of the Nutshell Handbooks, *Managing UUCP and Usenet* and *Using UUCP and Usenet*.

John Strang now finds himself "a consumer--rather than a producer of Nutshells." He is currently a diagnostic radiologist (MD) at Stanford University. He is married to a pediatrician, Susie, and they have two children, Katie and Alex. John enjoys hiking, bicycling, and dabbling in other sciences. He plans to use his experience as an author at ORA to write his own book on radiology.

Jerry Peek has used UNIX since the early 1980's. He has a B.S. in Electronic Engineering Technology from California Polytechnic State University, San Luis Obispo. At Syracuse University, Jerry was a user consultant for UNIX and VMS. At Tektronix, Inc., he was a UNIX a course developer and trainer; a System Administrator of a VAX 11/780 running BSD UNIX; and a Bourne Shell and C language job-shop programmer. Jerry is currently a user consultant and writer for O'Reilly & Associates, Inc.

Colophon

Our look is the result of reader comments, our own experimentation, and distribution channels.

Distinctive covers complement our distinctive approach to technical topics, breathing personality and life into potentially dry subjects. UNIX and its attendant programs can be unruly beasts. Nutshell Handbooks help you tame them.

The animal featured on the cover of *Learning the UNIX Operating System* is the horned owl. The horned owl is the most powerful of the North American owls, measuring from 18 to 25 inches long. This nocturnal bird of prey feeds exclusively on animals—primarily rabbits, rodents, and birds, including other owls—which it locates by sound rather than sight, its night vision being little better than ours. To aid in its hunting, an owl has very soft feathers which muffle the sound of its motion, making it virtually silent in flight. A tree-dwelling bird, it generally chooses to inhabit the old nests of other large birds such as hawks and crows rather than build its own nest.

Edie Freedman designed this cover and the entire UNIX bestiary that appears on other Nutshell Handbooks. The beasts themselves are adapted from 19th-century engravings from the Dover Pictorial Archive. Whenever possible, our books use RepKover™, a durable and flexible lay-flat binding. If the page count exceeds RepKover's limit, perfect binding is used.

The text of this book is set in ITC Garamond and Courier. The text pages are formatted in troff. Figures were created by Chris Reilley in Aldus Freehand. The cover was produced in QuarkXPress.

sed & awk, 2nd Edition

By Dale Dougherty & Arnold Robbins
2nd Edition Winter 1997
450 pages (est.), ISBN 1-56592-225-5

sed & awk, one of the most popular
books in O'Reilly & Associates' Nutshell
series, describes two text processing
programs that are mainstays of the UNIX
programmer's toolbox. The book lays a
foundation for both programs by describing how they are
used and by introducing the fundamental concepts of regular
expressions and text matching. This new edition covers the
sed and *awk* programs as they are now mandated by the
POSIX standard. It also includes a discussion of the GNU versions of both programs, which have extensions beyond their
UNIX counterparts. Many examples are used throughout the
book to illustrate the concepts discussed.

SCO UNIX in a Nutshell

By Ellie Cutler & the staff of O'Reilly &
Associates
1st Edition February 1994
590 pages, ISBN 1-56592-037-6

The desktop reference to SCO UNIX and
Open Desktop®, this version of *UNIX in
a Nutshell* shows you what's under the
hood of your SCO system. It isn't a
scaled-down quick reference of com-
mon commands, but a complete reference containing all
user, programming, administration, and networking commands.

UNIX in a Nutshell: System V Edition

By Daniel Gilly &
the staff of O'Reilly & Associates
2nd Edition June 1992
444 pages, ISBN 1-56592-001-5

You may have seen UNIX quick-reference guides, but you've never seen anything like *UNIX in a Nutshell*. Not a
scaled-down quick reference of common commands, *UNIX in a Nutshell* is a
complete reference containing all com-
mands and options, along with generous descriptions and
examples that put the commands in context. For all but the
thorniest UNIX problems, this one reference should be all the
documentation you need. Covers System V, Releases 3 and 4,
and Solaris 2.0.

What You Need to Know: When You Can't Find Your UNIX System Administrator

By Linda Mui
1st Edition April 1995
156 pages, ISBN 1-56592-104-6

This book is written for UNIX users,
who are often cast adrift in a confusing
environment. It provides the background and practical solutions you need
to solve problems you're likely to
encounter—problems with logging in, printing, sharing files,
running programs, managing space resources, etc. It also
describes the kind of info to gather when you're asking for a
diagnosis from a busy sys admin. And, it gives you a list of
site-specific information that you should know, as well as a
place to write it down.

Volume 3M: X Window System User's Guide, Motif Edition

By Valerie Quercia & Tim O'Reilly
2nd Edition January 1993
956 pages, ISBN 1-56592-015-5

The *X Window System User's Guide,
Motif Edition* orients the new user to
window system concepts and provides detailed tutorials for many
client programs, including the
xtermterminal emulator and the twm,
uwm, and mwmwindow managers. Later chapters explain
how to customize the X environment. Revised for Motif 1.2
and X11 Release 5.

O'REILLY™

TO ORDER: **800-998-9938** • *order@oreilly.com* • *http://www.oreilly.com/*
OUR PRODUCTS ARE AVAILABLE AT A BOOKSTORE OR SOFTWARE STORE NEAR YOU.
FOR INFORMATION: **800-998-9938** • **707-829-0515** • *info@oreilly.com*

Internet for Everyone

The Whole Internet User's Guide & Catalog

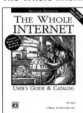

By Ed Krol
2nd Edition April 1994
574 pages, ISBN 1-56592-063-5

Still the best book on the Internet. This is the second edition of our comprehensive introduction to the Internet. An international network that includes virtually every major computer site in the world, the Internet is a resource of almost unimaginable wealth. In addition to the World Wide Web, electronic mail, and news services, thousands of public archives, databases, and other special services are available. This book covers Internet basics—like email, file transfer, remote login, and network news. Useful to beginners and veterans alike, also includes a pull-out quick-reference card.

The Whole Internet for Windows 95

By Ed Krol & Paula Ferguson
1st Edition October 1995
650 pages, ISBN 1-56592-155-0

The Whole Internet for Windows 95, the most comprehensive introduction to the Internet available today, shows you how to take advantage of the vast resources of the Internet with Microsoft Internet Explorer, Netscape Navigator, Microsoft Exchange, and many of the best free software programs available from the Net. Also includes an introduction to multimedia for PCs and a catalog of interesting sites to explore.

Bandits on the Information Superhighway

By Daniel J. Barrett
1st Edition February 1996
246 pages, ISBN 1-56592-156-9

Most people on the Internet behave honestly, but there are always some troublemakers. *Bandits* provides a crash course in Internet "street smarts," describing practical risks that every user should know about. Filled with anecdotes, technical tips, and the advice of experts from diverse fields, *Bandits* helps you identify and avoid risks online, so you can have a more productive and enjoyable time on the Internet.

Smileys

By David W. Sanderson
1st Edition March 1993
93 pages, ISBN 1-56592-041-4

From the people who put an armadillo on the cover of a system administrator book comes this collection of the computer underground hieroglyphs called "smileys." Originally inserted into email messages to denote "said with a cynical smile" :-) , smileys now run rampant throughout the electronic mail culture. They include references to politics 7:^] (Ronald Reagan), entertainment C]:-= (Charlie Chaplin), history 4:-) (George Washington), and mythology @-) (cyclops). They can laugh out loud %-(I) wink ;-) yell :-(0) frown :-(and even drool :-)~

Developing Web Content

WebMaster in a Nutshell, Deluxe Edition

By O'Reilly & Associates, Inc.
1st Edition September 1997 (est.)
356 pages (est.), includes CD-ROM
ISBN 1-56592-305-7

The Deluxe Edition of *WebMaster in a Nutshell* is a complete library for web programmers. The main resource is the Web Developer's Library, a CD-ROM, containing the electronic text of five popular O'Reilly titles: *HTML: The Definitive Guide, 2nd Edition*; *JavaScript: The Definitive Guide, 2nd Edition*; *CGI Programming on the World Wide Web*; *Programming Perl, 2nd Edition*—the classic "camel book," written by Larry Wall (the inventor of Perl) with Tom Christiansen and Randal Schwartz; and *WebMaster in a Nutshell*. The Deluxe Edition also includes a printed copy of *WebMaster in a Nutshell*.

WebMaster in a Nutshell, Deluxe Edition, makes it easy to find the information you need with all of the convenience you'd expect from the Web. You'll have access to information webmasters and programmers use most for development—complete with global searching and a master index to all five volumes—all on a single CD-ROM. It's incredibly portable. Just slip it into your laptop case as you commute or take off on your next trip and you'll find everything at your fingertips with no books to carry.

The CD-ROM is readable on all hardware platforms. All files except Java code example files are in 8.3 file format and, therefore, are readable by older systems. A web browser that supports HTML 3.2 (such as Netscape 3.0 or Internet Explorer 3.0) is required to view the text. The browser must support Java if searching is desired.

The Web Developer's Library is also available by subscription on the World Wide Web. See http://www.ora.com/catalog/webrlw for details.

WebMaster in a Nutshell

By Stephen Spainhour & Valerie Quercia
1st Edition October 1996
374 pages, ISBN 1-56592-229-8

Web content providers and administrators have many sources for information, both in print and online. *WebMaster in a Nutshell* puts it all together in one slim volume for easy desktop access. This quick reference covers HTML, CGI, JavaScript, Perl, HTTP, and server configuration.

HTML: The Definitive Guide, 2nd Edition

By Chuck Musciano & Bill Kennedy
2nd Edition May 1997
552 pages, ISBN 1-56592-235-2

This complete guide is chock full of examples, sample code, and practical, hands-on advice to help you create truly effective web pages and master advanced features. Learn how to insert images and other multimedia elements, create useful links and searchable documents, use Netscape extensions, design great forms, and lots more. The second edition covers the most up-to-date version of the HTML standard (HTML version 3.2), Netscape 4.0 and Internet Explorer 3.0, plus all the common extensions.

JavaScript: The Definitive Guide, 2nd Edition

By David Flanagan
2nd Edition January 1997
664 pages, ISBN 1-56592-234-4

This second edition of the definitive reference guide to JavaScript, the HTML extension that gives web pages programming-language capabilities, covers JavaScript as it is used in Netscape 3.0 and 2.0 and in Microsoft Internet Explorer 3.0. Learn how JavaScript really works (and when it doesn't). Use JavaScript to control web browser behavior, add dynamically created text to web pages, interact with users through HTML forms, and even control and interact with Java applets and Navigator plug-ins. By the author of the bestselling *Java in a Nutshell*.

O'REILLY™

TO ORDER: **800-998-9938** • **order@oreilly.com** • **http://www.oreilly.com/**
OUR PRODUCTS ARE AVAILABLE AT A BOOKSTORE OR SOFTWARE STORE NEAR YOU.
FOR INFORMATION: **800-998-9938** • **707-829-0515** • **info@oreilly.com**

Developing Web Content *continued*

GI Programming on the World Wide Web

By Shishir Gundavaram
1st Edition March 1996
450 pages, ISBN: 1-56592-168-2

This book offers a comprehensive explanation of CGI and related techniques for people who hold on to the dream of providing their own information servers on the Web. It starts at the beginning, explaining the value of CGI and how it works, then moves swiftly into the subtle details of programming.

Information Architecture for the World Wide Web

By Louis Rosenfeld & Peter Morville
1st Edition November 1997 (est.)
200 pages (est.), ISBN 1-56592-282-4

Information Architecture for the World Wide Web is about applying the principles of architecture and library science to web site design. With this book, you learn how to design web sites and intranets that support growth, management, and ease of use. This book is for webmasters, designers, and anyone else involved in building a web site.

Learning VBScript

By Paul Lomax
1st Edition July 1997
616 pages, includes CD-ROM
ISBN 1-56592-247-6

This definitive guide shows web developers how to take full advantage of client-side scripting with the VBScript language. In addition to basic language features, it covers the Internet Explorer object model and discusses techniques for client-side scripting, like adding ActiveX controls to a web page or validating data before sending it to the server. Includes CD-ROM with over 170 code samples.

Web Client Programming with Perl

By Clinton Wong
1st Edition March 1997
228 pages, ISBN 1-56592-214-X

Web Client Programming with Perl shows you how to extend scripting skills to the Web. This book teaches you the basics of how browsers communicate with servers and how to write your own customized web clients to automate common tasks. It is intended for those who are motivated to develop software that offers a more flexible and dynamic response than a standard web browser.

Building Your Own WebSite

By Susan B. Peck & Stephen Arrants
1st Edition July 1996
514 pages, ISBN 1-56592-232-8

This is a hands-on reference for Windows® 95 and Windows NT™ users who want to host a site on the Web or on a corporate intranet. This step-by-step guide will have you creating live web pages in minutes.

You'll also learn how to connect your web to information in other Windows applications, such as word processing documents and databases. The book is packed with examples and tutorials on every aspect of web management, and it includes the highly acclaimed WebSite™ 1.1 server software on CD-ROM.

Designing for the Web: Getting Started in a New Medium

By Jennifer Niederst
with Edie Freedman
1st Edition April 1996
180 pages, ISBN 1-56592-165-8

Designing for the Web gives you the basics you need to hit the ground running. Although geared toward designers, it covers information and techniques useful to anyone who wants to put graphics online. It explains how to work with HTML documents from a designer's point of view, outlines special problems with presenting information online, and walks through incorporating images into web pages, with emphasis on resolution and improving efficiency.

O'REILLY™

TO ORDER: **800-998-9938** • *order@oreilly.com* • *http://www.oreilly.com/*
OUR PRODUCTS ARE AVAILABLE AT A BOOKSTORE OR SOFTWARE STORE NEAR YOU.
FOR INFORMATION: **800-998-9938** • **707-829-0515** • *info@oreilly.com*

How to stay in touch with O'Reilly

1. Visit Our Award-Winning Site

http://www.oreilly.com/

★"Top 100 Sites on the Web" —*PC Magazine*
★"Top 5% Web sites" —*Point Communications*
★"3-Star site" —*The McKinley Group*

Our web site contains a library of comprehensive product information (including book excerpts and tables of contents), downloadable software, background articles, interviews with technology leaders, links to relevant sites, book cover art, and more. File us in your Bookmarks or Hotlist!

2. Join Our Email Mailing Lists

New Product Releases

To receive automatic email with brief descriptions of all new O'Reilly products as they are released, send email to:
listproc@online.oreilly.com
Put the following information in the first line of your message (*not* in the Subject field):
subscribe oreilly-news "Your Name" of "Your Organization" (for example: subscribe oreilly-news Kris Webber of Fine Enterprises)

O'Reilly Events

If you'd also like us to send information about trade show events, special promotions, and other O'Reilly events, send email to:
listproc@online.oreilly.com
Put the following information in the first line of your message (*not* in the Subject field):
subscribe oreilly-events "Your Name" of "Your Organization"

3. Get Examples from Our Books via FTP

There are two ways to access an archive of example files from our books:

Regular FTP

* ftp to:
  ftp.oreilly.com
  (login: anonymous
  password: your email address)
* Point your web browser to:
  ftp://ftp.oreilly.com/

FTPMAIL

* Send an email message to:
  ftpmail@online.oreilly.com
  (Write "help" in the message body)

4. Visit Our Gopher Site

* Connect your gopher to:
  gopher.oreilly.com

* Point your web browser to:
  gopher://gopher.oreilly.com/

* Telnet to:
  gopher.oreilly.com
  login: gopher

5. Contact Us via Email

order@oreilly.com
To place a book or software order online. Good for North American and international customers.

subscriptions@oreilly.com
To place an order for any of our newsletters or periodicals.

books@oreilly.com
General questions about any of our books.

software@oreilly.com
For general questions and product information about our software. Check out O'Reilly Software Online at **http://software.oreilly.com/** for software and technical support information. Registered O'Reilly software users send your questions to:
website-support@oreilly.com

cs@oreilly.com
For answers to problems regarding your order or our products.

booktech@oreilly.com
For book content technical questions or corrections.

proposals@oreilly.com
To submit new book or software proposals to our editors and product managers.

international@oreilly.com
For information about our international distributors or translation queries. For a list of our distributors outside of North America check out:
http://www.oreilly.com/www/order/country.html

O'Reilly & Associates, Inc.
101 Morris Street, Sebastopol, CA 95472 USA
TEL   707-829-0515 or 800-998-9938
      (6am to 5pm PST)
FAX   707-829-0104

O'REILLY™

TO ORDER: **800-998-9938** • *order@oreilly.com* • *http://www.oreilly.com/*
OUR PRODUCTS ARE AVAILABLE AT A BOOKSTORE OR SOFTWARE STORE NEAR YOU.
FOR INFORMATION: **800-998-9938** • **707-829-0515** • *info@oreilly.com*

Titles from O'Reilly

Please note that upcoming titles are displayed in italic.

WEB PROGRAMMING

Apache: The Definitive Guide
Building Your Own Web
  Conferences
Building Your Own Website
Building Your Own Win-CGI
  Programs
CGI Programming for the World
  Wide Web
Designing for the Web
HTML: The Definitive Guide
JavaScript: The Definitive Guide,
  2nd Ed.
Learning Perl
Programming Perl, 2nd Ed.
Mastering Regular Expressions
WebMaster in a Nutshell
Web Security & Commerce
*Web Client Programming with
  Perl*
World Wide Web Journal

USING THE INTERNET

Smileys
The Future Does Not Compute
The Whole Internet User's Guide
  & Catalog
The Whole Internet for Win 95
Using Email Effectively
Bandits on the Information
  Superhighway

JAVA SERIES

Exploring Java
Java AWT Reference
Java Fundamental Classes
  Reference
Java in a Nutshell
Java Language Reference
Java Network Programming
Java Threads
Java Virtual Machine

SOFTWARE

WebSite™ 1.1
WebSite Professional™
Building Your Own Web
  Conferences
WebBoard™
PolyForm™
Statisphere™

SONGLINE GUIDES

NetActivism   NetResearch
Net Law   NetSuccess
NetLearning   NetTravel
Net Lessons

SYSTEM ADMINISTRATION

Building Internet Firewalls
Computer Crime: A Crimefighter's
  Handbook
Computer Security Basics
DNS and BIND, 2nd Ed.
Essential System Administration,
  2nd Ed.
Getting Connected: The Internet
  at 56K and Up
*Internet Server Administration
  with Windows NT*
Linux Network Administrator's
  Guide
Managing Internet Information
  Services
Managing NFS and NIS
Networking Personal Computers
  with TCP/IP
Practical UNIX & Internet
  Security, 2nd Ed.
PGP: Pretty Good Privacy
sendmail, 2nd Ed.
sendmail Desktop Reference
System Performance Tuning
TCP/IP Network Administration
termcap & terminfo
Using & Managing UUCP
Volume 8: X Window System
  Administrator's Guide
Web Security & Commerce

UNIX

Exploring Expect
Learning VBScript
Learning GNU Emacs, 2nd Ed.
Learning the bash Shell
Learning the Korn Shell
Learning the UNIX Operating
  System
Learning the vi Editor
Linux in a Nutshell
Making TeX Work
Linux Multimedia Guide
Running Linux, 2nd Ed.
SCO UNIX in a Nutshell
sed & awk, 2nd Edition
Tcl/Tk Tools
UNIX in a Nutshell: System V
  Edition
UNIX Power Tools
Using csh & tcsh
When You Can't Find Your UNIX
  System Administrator
Writing GNU Emacs Extensions

WEB REVIEW STUDIO SERIES

Gif Animation Studio
Shockwave Studio

WINDOWS

Dictionary of PC Hardware and
  Data Communications Terms
Inside the Windows 95 Registry
Inside the Windows 95 File
  System
Windows Annoyances
*Windows NT File System
  Internals*
Windows NT in a Nutshell

PROGRAMMING

Advanced Oracle PL/SQL
  Programming
Applying RCS and SCCS
C++: The Core Language
Checking C Programs with lint
DCE Security Programming
Distributing Applications Across
  DCE & Windows NT
Encyclopedia of Graphics File
  Formats, 2nd Ed.
Guide to Writing DCE
  Applications
lex & yacc
Managing Projects with make
Mastering Oracle Power Objects
Oracle Design: The Definitive
  Guide
Oracle Performance Tuning, 2nd
  Ed.
Oracle PL/SQL Programming
Porting UNIX Software
POSIX Programmer's Guide
POSIX.4: Programming for the
  Real World
Power Programming with RPC
Practical C Programming
Practical C++ Programming
Programming Python
Programming with curses
Programming with GNU Software
Pthreads Programming
Software Portability with imake,
  2nd Ed.
Understanding DCE
Understanding Japanese
  Information Processing
UNIX Systems Programming for
  SVR4

BERKELEY 4.4 SOFTWARE
DISTRIBUTION

4.4BSD System Manager's Manual
4.4BSD User's Reference Manual
4.4BSD User's Supplementary
  Documents
4.4BSD Programmer's Reference
  Manual
4.4BSD Programmer's
  Supplementary Documents
X Programming
Vol. 0: X Protocol Reference
  Manual
Vol. 1: Xlib Programming Manual
Vol. 2: Xlib Reference Manual
Vol. 3M: X Window System User's
  Guide, Motif Edition
Vol. 4M: X Toolkit Intrinsics
  Programming Manual, Motif
  Edition
Vol. 5: X Toolkit Intrinsics
  Reference Manual
Vol. 6A: Motif Programming
  Manual
Vol. 6B: Motif Reference Manual
Vol. 6C: Motif Tools
Vol. 8 : X Window System
  Administrator's Guide
Programmer's Supplement for
  Release 6
X User Tools
The X Window System in a
  Nutshell

CAREER & BUSINESS

Building a Successful Software
  Business
The Computer User's Survival
  Guide
Love Your Job!
Electronic Publishing on CD-ROM

TRAVEL

Travelers' Tales: Brazil
Travelers' Tales: Food
Travelers' Tales: France
Travelers' Tales: Gutsy Women
Travelers' Tales: India
Travelers' Tales: Mexico
Travelers' Tales: Paris
Travelers' Tales: San Francisco
Travelers' Tales: Spain
Travelers' Tales: Thailand
Travelers' Tales: A Woman's
  World

O'REILLY™

TO ORDER: **800-998-9938** • **order@oreilly.com** • **http://www.oreilly.com/**

OUR PRODUCTS ARE AVAILABLE AT A BOOKSTORE OR SOFTWARE STORE NEAR YOU.

FOR INFORMATION: **800-998-9938** • **707-829-0515** • **info@oreilly.com**

International Distributors

UK, Europe, Middle East and Northern Africa (except France, Germany, Switzerland, & Austria)

INQUIRIES
International Thomson Publishing Europe
Berkshire House
168-173 High Holborn
London WC1V 7AA, UK
Tel: 44-171-497-1422
Fax: 44-171-497-1426
Email: itpint@itps.co.uk

ORDERS
International Thomson Publishing Services, Ltd.
Cheriton House, North Way
Andover, Hampshire SP10 5BE,
United Kingdom
Tel: 44-264-342-832 (UK)
Tel: 44-264-342-806
  (outside UK)
Fax: 44-264-364418 (UK)
Fax: 44-264-342761 (outside UK)
UK & Eire orders:
itpuk@itps.co.uk
International orders:
itpint@itps.co.uk

France

Editions Eyrolles
61 bd Saint-Germain
75240 Paris Cedex 05
France
Fax: 33-01-44-41-11-44

FRENCH LANGUAGE BOOKS
All countries except Canada
Tel: 33-01-44-41-46-16
Email: geodif@eyrolles.com

ENGLISH LANGUAGE BOOKS
Tel: 33-01-44-41-11-87
Email: distribution@eyrolles.com

Australia

WoodsLane Pty. Ltd.
7/5 Vuko Place, Warriewood NSW 2102
P.O. Box 935,
Mona Vale NSW 2103
Australia
Tel: 61-2-9970-5111
Fax: 61-2-9970-5002
Email: info@woodslane.com.au

Germany, Switzerland, and Austria

INQUIRIES
O'Reilly Verlag
Balthasarstr. 81
D-50670 Köln
Germany
Tel: 49-221-97-31-60-0
Fax: 49-221-97-31-60-8
Email: anfragen@oreilly.de

ORDERS
International Thomson Publishing
Königswinterer Straße 418
53227 Bonn, Germany
Tel: 49-228-97024 0
Fax: 49-228-441342
Email: order@oreilly.de

Asia (except Japan & India)

INQUIRIES
International Thomson Publishing Asia
60 Albert Street #15-01
Albert Complex
Singapore 189969
Tel: 65-336-6411
Fax: 65-336-7411

ORDERS
Telephone: 65-336-6411
Fax: 65-334-1617
thomson@signet.com.sg

New Zealand

WoodsLane New Zealand Ltd.
21 Cooks Street (P.O. Box 575)
Wanganui, New Zealand
Tel: 64-6-347-6543
Fax: 64-6-345-4840
Email: info@woodslane.com.au

Japan

O'Reilly Japan, Inc.
Kiyoshige Building 2F
12-Banchi, Sanei-cho
Shinjuku-ku
Tokyo 160 Japan
Tel: 81-3-3356-5227
Fax: 81-3-3356-5261
Email: kenji@oreilly.com

India

Computer Bookshop (India) PVT. LTD.
190 Dr. D.N. Road, Fort
Bombay 400 001 India
Tel: 91-22-207-0989
Fax: 91-22-262-3551
Email:
cbsbom@giasbm01.vsnl.net.in

The Americas

O'Reilly & Associates, Inc.
101 Morris Street
Sebastopol, CA 95472 U.S.A.
Tel: 707-829-0515
Tel: 800-998-9938 (U.S. & Canada)
Fax: 707-829-0104
Email: order@oreilly.com

Southern Africa

International Thomson Publishing Southern Africa
Building 18, Constantia Park
138 Sixteenth Road
P.O. Box 2459
Halfway House, 1685 South Africa
Tel: 27-11-805-4819
Fax: 27-11-805-3648

O'REILLY™